The new psychology for leadership

Books by Donald A. Laird and Eleanor C. Laird

THE NEW PSYCHOLOGY FOR LEADERSHIP

PRACTICAL SALES PSYCHOLOGY

PRACTICAL BUSINESS PSYCHOLOGY *Revised Edition*

SIZING UP PEOPLE

THE TECHNIQUE OF GETTING THINGS DONE

THE TECHNIQUE OF PERSONAL ANALYSIS

THE TECHNIQUE OF BUILDING PERSONAL LEADERSHIP

THE TECHNIQUE OF HANDLING PEOPLE *Revised Edition*

THE PSYCHOLOGY OF SELECTING EMPLOYEES

Published by Harper & Brothers
INCREASING PERSONAL EFFICIENCY

Published by Funk & Wagnalls Company
THE STRATEGY OF HANDLING CHILDREN

Published by American Bankers Association
HUMAN RELATIONS IN BANKING

The new psychology for leadership

BASED ON RESEARCHES IN GROUP DYNAMICS AND HUMAN RELATIONS.... *by*

Dr. Donald A. Laird and Eleanor C. Laird

McGRAW-HILL BOOK COMPANY, INC.   *New York*

Toronto   London

/

150.13
Lai

THE NEW PSYCHOLOGY FOR LEADERSHIP

Copyright © 1956 by the McGraw-Hill Book Company, Inc. Printed in the United States of America. All rights reserved. This book, or parts thereof, may not be reproduced in any form without permission of the publishers.

Library of Congress Catalog Card Number: 55–12106

400
B&T

Contents

1   *The new guides for leaders*

Each year more organizations are making greater effort to increase their executives' know-how for dealing with the human-relations aspects of leadership. This steadily growing emphasis on workable human relations is due largely to the rapid development of new research which is showing what works, what doesn't—and why.

This research on human relations in leadership comes chiefly from some two dozen specialized research centers in the U.S. The armed forces, in addition, have their own research installations which are gathering and evaluating more facts about the human-relations angles of leadership. During recent years these civilian and military centers have been researching at the rate of at least six million dollars a year.

All this activity uncovers, in a single year, more down-to-earth facts about leadership than was uncovered during the entire century following Abraham Lincoln. An entirely new conception of leadership has emerged from the findings of these research teams. This new slant on leadership makes the old inspirational maxims about "how to be a leader" as obsolete as a quill pen.

But as the research has grown, it has become more and more technical. New terms have been invented, and old words have been given new meanings. As a consequence, the average executive or supervisor often can't figure out what it is all about. We hope this book will fill the gap.

We are giving accounts of some of the basic findings from 22 research centers. The technical terms are left out, and replaced by words from everyday and business life. The reports included are typical of the trends, and deal mostly with face-to-face leadership at the first level.

Most of the findings we will explain are from actual office, factory, and military situations. Sometimes the workers did not realize they were guinea pigs. Business went on as usual while records were collected about production, absences, cost consciousness, grievances, group pride, prejudice, grapevine gossip, job details, interest in the work, and other natural variations.

There are some practical leadership questions which cannot safely be experimented with in an ongoing organization. Such as what might happen if one member of a crew whispers to others to "slow down." (Answer: They slowed down, from 12 per cent to 20 per cent.) Laboratory type studies have proven useful to answer questions of this "touchy" type, and some will be included in this book.

The findings reported have high trustworthiness. We give only cases where the trends shown have at least 95 chances out of 100 of being true and not due to luck.

To be certain that the simplified chartoons give the gist accurately, we have asked a senior member of each research team to check the drawing and accompanying text. We extend sincere thanks for this cooperation from time-pressed men and women. Our part has been merely to tie the researchers' findings together, and point out how the active leader can be guided by these findings.

What human relations are

It is natural to assume that human relations means be nice to others. But human relations goes much deeper than spasms of good will.

As research on the interactions between people, and between followers and their leaders has advanced, it has become apparent that there are three prime considerations:

1. Anxiety
2. Hostility
3. Group forces

Human relations can be described as understanding (know-why) and working with (know-how) the mental and social forces in a group of people, so that hostile feelings are kept under control and anxiety is kept at a minimum. Like most broad statements, that is vague. So, let's look further into it.

When a worker is given praise, or criticism, some mental forces are touched off inside his head. Praise touches off different forces than criticism does. Not much hostility or anxiety should be expected from praise.

But social forces also modify the worker's reactions to, say, criticism. If he is criticized in front of his friends, he will take it differently than if his friends knew nothing about it. If he is criticized for something his friends approve, say, like taking time out for a smoke, he will respond pretty much as if his friends were right at his elbow. Social forces are involved, even though the group may be out of sight at the time.

The leader who is good in his human relations methods has a pretty sound idea about how Joe Spank (and others in Joe's groups) are going to feel, and act, about what the

leader does. Will they feel cooperative or hostile if he sim-
plifies the work for them? If he fails to get the higher-ups
to O.K. something he promised his crew? Or if he tries to
win an argument by beating them to the draw? (In each of
those instances the leader will likely get hostile feelings and
anxiety, topped by a slump in productivity, as will be illustrated in detail shortly.)

How people will feel and act toward others, and toward
the leader, is the underlying practical question. These interactions between people go on in a sort of endless chain. One
interaction leads to another. These chain interactions explain
why seemingly simple actions by the leader produce unex-
pected consequences in human relations. Such as why nearly
half of factory workers deliberately hold down their output,
even when on incentive-payment rates. Or why some legisla-
tion which was aimed to cramp labor unions seems actually
to increase union membership.

Which way the chain of interactions develops often depends upon social or group forces which the leader may have
overlooked.

How group affiliations alter human relations

A clear-cut example is found in the way various groups of
people feel about evading regulations. Dr. Erwin O. Smigel
has studied this, with the support of a research grant from the
Graduate School of Indiana University (111).*

Typical chiseling incidents were described to adults, to get
their attitudes toward chiseling on unemployment compensa-

---

* The numbers in parentheses refer to the original report in the list of
sources cited, which starts on page 207.

tion. One incident: "Jack Green quit his job to take a rest he felt he needed. The foreman was a friend of his and gave Jack a slip saying he had been laid off. Jack took the slip and

"Chiseling" on compensation was approved by more of those of low occupational status

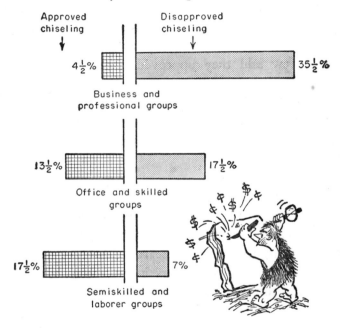

Approved
chiseling

Disapproved
chiseling

$4\frac{1}{2}\%$ $35\frac{1}{2}\%$

Business and
professional groups

$13\frac{1}{2}\%$ $17\frac{1}{2}\%$

Office and skilled
groups

$17\frac{1}{2}\%$ 7%

Semiskilled and
laborer groups

applied for unemployment compensation, which was given him."

On the average, only 7 per cent approved of Jack's chiseling.

But in the case of Dan Smith who chiseled by pretending he had poor health, 25 per cent approved. This greater approval of Dan reflects the inclination to be lenient when the case bears on a group ideal, such as taking care of the handicapped.

Of most interest to us at present is the way various occupational groups felt about the chiseling examples. This is shown in the chartoon. Note that the lower occupational groups showed most approval of this chiseling. This is only one of many examples of the way the interests of the groups to which one belongs shape the attitudes of the members.

Some of these adults did not realize that the chiseling was illegal. A few said they approved chiseling because they thought the money came from taxes taken from the chiseler. But there wasn't much change in attitudes when these people were told that the money was collected solely from the employers. Group loyalties are often stronger than logic.

*   *   *

Previous membership in a group may also carry over and influence the way the individual forms hostile or anxious attitudes from his interactions with others. This is illustrated by a study made by the Survey Research Center, of the University of Michigan, of supervisors in an automobile factory. Some of the foremen had previously been union stewards, others had not been stewards (117).

A significantly larger share of the former stewards thought of themselves as union men, and not primarily as company men.

*   *   *

The way a change of one's group affiliations shifts attitudes was demonstrated in an analysis by Dr. Seymour Lieberman of 2,500 blue-collar workers in a Middle Western factory. The psychologists had records of the attitudes of each of these men toward the union and toward the management. A year later the men who had been promoted to foremen, or elected stewards, were followed up (74).

The first discovery was that the men elected stewards had been no more pro-union than the rest, and that the men promoted to foremen had not been any more pro-management than the others. Even Stephen at the start.

The next discovery revealed that within a short time after the promotion, or election, the men's attitudes had "spontaneously" shifted. The newly elected stewards became much more pro-union than they had formerly been. The new foremen became much more pro-management than they had been a few months previously. The shifts in attitudes were larger, and more widespread, among the new foremen than among the new stewards.

The need of working with group forces

It would be helpful if the modern work force were "one big family." But it is usually a collection of people from overlapping groups. Employees are wrapped up in different community groups, such as lodges, churches, political parties, and recreation groups. Inside the company they group themselves together on such bases as kind of work, pay, education, car pool, or place of living. These overlapping, and at times conflicting affiliations, set the stage for chain interactions which may cause the well-intended efforts of the leaders to backfire.

Consider this boss who is talking alone with John Brown in a corner of the shop. The boss took Brown to one side to avoid group influences. It is not done that simply, however. Brown is not alone in that corner. He hears his group's voices. Not much chance to talk Brown into eating in the company cafeteria if he feels the people in the greasy spoon around the corner are "more his kind of people." But he won't say that is the reason; probably he doesn't even realize that is the reason he prefers to go around the corner for lunch.

Thus a person can be physically separated from his groups, but it is difficult to take the influence of his groups out of his thinking and actions. He is likely to feel a bit hostile toward both the attitudes and people of groups to which he does not belong. And to have some anxiety when he is around groups which he feels do not accept him at his sterling values.

As a consequence, there is not much chance to talk Brown into giving a new worker a favorable start, in case the new man belongs to a religion which happens to be at odds with Brown's own church group.

Or to lead Brown to use the safety goggles if his work group entertains the notion that goggles are sissy. Or to speed up his output if the voice of his work group whispers "don't be a rate-buster."

Brown himself is up against similar group forces when he goes home. He will have his hands full trying to keep his teen-age daughter from driving the family car, if her group of teen-age friends thinks she should have the right to use the car. His son is likely to place a higher value on what his pals think than on what his parents approve (101).

And so it goes. People in this modern age seem to be led more by the whispers of their groups than by the shouts of their official leaders (17, 105).

Some hints about successful ways of leading through group forces are given in the following examples. Group forces can seldom be evaded, but with skilled leadership they can be upgraded.

Results of training in human-relations methods

In the following examples the leaders had had considerable experience. Some of them were at a high level of command leadership. But they got better results after some new-style training in the new style of human relations for leadership. Their training was not in the form of pep talks or inspirational lectures or films. Those older forms of training have not been found to produce significant results, when it has been possible to measure the results. The new-style training methods will be described as we go along (129).

Let's start with resistance to changes. It is a rare leader who has not been up against stone-wall opposition, or indifference, when changes are proposed. We'll look into a case where the problem was to get workers to accept a change which would save the company money. It might also make the job monotonous, and possibly change the rate of pay. A tough bill to sell.

In this case, some of the supervisors had no training in upgrading group forces. They did "what came naturally to them"—presented the facts as favorably as possible, and tried to argue the men into accepting the new method proposed by the engineers.

The column on the right shows that, after a half hour of intense selling effort, the *un*trained leaders had converted only half of the work groups to agree to the change.

Contrast that with the column on the left, which shows that the supervisors who had been given only eight hours' training got much better results.

In addition, a walkout was proposed by 5 per cent of the

men under the untrained bosses, but by none under those with the training on how to conduct group conferences with workers on job problems.

Getting workers to accept an improved work method

Complete **or** partial acceptance:

95%

50%

TRAINED leaders

UNtrained leaders

Here is an outline of the points on which the trained leaders had been trained:

1. Present the problem, but not the proposed solution.
2. Get *each man* to suggest a solution.
3. Let each air his personal views, without arguing with him.

4. Answer questions, or refer to someone else in the group.
5. Be tolerant of their criticisms, without talking back.
6. Keep them talking with each other (interacting), on the problem . . .
7. . . . until they are ready to reach a group decision.

Those seven steps outline the know-how. In later chapters we will come to understand the know-why involved in each step. But for the time being, it will be helpful if you analyze each step to figure out how it helps one handle the hostility or anxiety which might be touched off when a change in method is proposed.

This demonstration of the benefits from training in human relations for leadership was reported by Dr. Norman R. F. Maier, from work with industrial supervisors (80).

Catching on to instructions was influenced by human relations

A large Middle Western factory used the Jennings Supervisory Analysis to spot their foremen's weakest points. The weakest turned out to be "not giving clear instructions." Then came "not being fair to the workers," followed by "not going to bat for the workers."

Training was then started for all foremen, concentrating on the three weakest points. The foremen got together in groups of 15 men, and devoted three conferences to each point.

To get most participation, and to let each man feel it was his conference, they were asked to propose problems related to the weak points, and to suggest solutions to the problems.

Before each meeting they were given typical cases to figure out—warming up before the session.

To boost group spirit (cohesiveness), the foremen were allowed to choose the other men they wanted to sit in with in each conference. No sore-thumb fellows to put a wet blanket over the sincere swapping of ideas. The groups were thus made up of men who felt they "belonged together."

Half a year after this rather brief training, the workers again reported on the same foremen. This shows how the 20 foremen whom management had found to be poorest in overall leadership had improved on the weakest points:

	Percentage before training	Percentage after training
"Gives clear instructions"	18	61
"Fair to workers"	19	49

The gain in "giving clear instructions" appears to be the greater, but that may be misleadingly high. This is because of an important human-relations reaction, or interaction, which is worth understanding. It hinges upon hostility.

It probably did become easier for workers *to understand* instructions, even when the instructions were not given any more clearly by the foremen. People often show hostility unintentionally by having trouble understanding what is said by a person they dislike, or by a person they feel represents a group that is at odds with some aims of their own groups. A large share of "denseness" in catching on to directions is just a hostile interaction.

Understanding instructions is not all a question of plain language in communicating the facts. Hostility can throw a roadblock across the clearest of instructions. Communicating is a human-relations problem as well as a problem in the clear expression of ideas.

This is how it probably worked out in this factory. The training produced some changes in the foremen so they became less likely to touch off hostility. Then it became easier to understand instructions. Another illustration of chain actions in mental and social forces.

A less favorable example of chain actions is that these workers reported no improvement in their foremen's going to bat for them. The company was set up so that all grievances by-passed the foremen. Company procedures sometimes erect roadblocks which weaken the leadership of the first line.

This research was done from the Bureau of Business Research and Service, of the University of Wisconsin, by Dr. Eugene E. Jennings, who is now with the Michigan State University (55).

Attitudes toward company profits

Which do you think would be the better way to lead employees to feel the profits were fair: Give them a heart-to-heart talk on company finances and earnings? Or "humanize" their bosses with some human-relations training?

A demonstration of how the "human climate" seemed to outweigh the economic facts of life was made by Drs. Norman R. F. Maier and Allen R. Solem, of the University of Michigan. They compared the effects of the two methods on 175 supervisors of one firm who played the roles of workers of another company (81).

The Other Company was a family-owned money-maker. The founder's son, who was pictured as president, spent most of his time in high society. The foremen reportedly watched workers closely to see that there was no loafing. This Other Company paid average wages according to local standards, but the local average was low.

What made more of them think the company deserved more profit

The column on the left of this chartoon shows that, after that description, only 29 per cent of the foremen felt the Other Company was justified in making more than 6 per cent on its investment.

Then these supervisors heard a high executive recite the history of the company and the struggles of its small beginning. He used charts to explain how their profits and pay schedules were fair. A short movie showed how workers were trained, and illustrated their retirement benefits.

The middle column shows that this straightforward talk led an appreciable share to shift their profit attitudes in a direction that was *un*favorable to the company. The talk aroused mistrust (hostility), as many lectures do, when brain-washing is suspected. The people in one group (workers in this case) are likely to raise their guard when they sense that another group (the management in this case) is trying to change the opinions of the one group. In such fashion, a direct attack on the beliefs of the one group may set up a chain of interactions which puts a wider gap between the two groups. Finding fault with one thing is often an indirect way of manifesting hostility which is actually owing to something else.

Clearing up some of this underlying hostility will often alter the other attitudes. This is shown by the column on the right. This pictures the way attitudes toward company earnings became more favorable after the men were told that the style of the foremen had been improved. The foremen had been trained so that they asked for workers' ideas about job procedures, instead of mainly policing the workers. The bosses had quit bawling the men out, and began trying to help them solve troubles, both personal troubles and job troubles.

Experienced Air Force leaders benefited

The examples so far have dealt with first-line leaders. How about leaders at higher levels, who have administrative and policy-making responsibilities? Face-to-face leadership pre-dominates at the first line, but is usually less needed at the higher levels.

An answer comes from work with 400 majors and lieu-tenant colonels of the U.S. Air Force. This study was made at the Air University, by Dr. Irving Lorge and staff members of the Institute of Psychological Research of Teachers College, at Columbia University (78).

Before taking the special training, these experienced officers did their best to solve such practical problems as: "What would be the best ways to prevent, or cure, poor morale among airmen at an isolated outpost in the Arctic?" Small committees of these officers wrote out staff reports of their recommendations.

Then the same officers had a six months' course in group problem solving. After this training, they went into con-ference again and made staff recommendations on assorted human-relations problems to be dealt with in the Air Force. Here is how their "before" and "after" recommendations stacked up:

	Before training	After training
Quality of decisions on practical human-relations problems	13	24

In addition, the "after" reports contained 71 per cent more general recommendations. There were also six times as many specific suggestions.

The overwhelming superiority of the "after" decisions is partly owing to the added facts they had picked up from the course, and also from interactions with other officers in the conference groups.

The "after" decisions were greatly strengthened because the officers had learned how to give and take ideas without fighting back (hostility) to defend their own first ideas. This is an important virtue in such "group thinks"—as individuals become more skilled in producing smoother interactions with others, there is less inclination to strut like prima donnas and argue pointlessly. As the interactions in the planning group become free and easy, it is possible to use the full resources of all the group to catch the bugs in a plan—less blocking, or "misunderstanding" from hostile impulses.

The "after" decisions were also probably strengthened as the committees became more cohesive. As groups work together for some common purpose, they usually develop a cohesiveness, or mutual magnetism. Without cohesiveness, it would be merely a collection of people, not an integrated working group that pulls together. Cohesiveness makes the individuals feel "they belong," and they "open up" rather than "freeze up"—think constructively for the group's purpose rather than defensively. Cohesive groups appear to stimulate the thinking of individual members (20).

How the deck has been stacked for you

The central problem facing one leader may be a prejudice of one department, or group, against another. Slow-down tactics may give the next leader his biggest headache. With another it may be a poor safety record, clock-watching, or bickering between representatives of rival groups on the board of directors. And so on. Which should be taken up first as we get down to brass tacks?

It seems that there will be most long-run usefulness if the

findings are presented in an order to develop some working concepts, or general guides to mental and social forces. Just as the trained engineer has first to grasp the concepts of torque, hysteresis, and other forces in materials. The practical mechanic, in contrast, jumps in feet-first to make the gadget right away, and may still think that hysteresis is what makes women cry over nothing.

The topics will be unfolded in this book in a way planned to build up a working grasp of some of the basic concepts in human relations and group dynamics. Some of the overlapping is unavoidable, some of it deliberate to provide an automatic review as you read along. The last capsule summary of research may turn out to be of most immediate help in some present problem, but you will likely make better application of it after the significant conceptions have grown on you.

In the following chapter we will take a close-up look at the quality of present-day leadership, at the first level mainly. In the third chapter we will get acquainted with two contrasted styles of leadership, and see the implications these styles have for the "human climate" in an ongoing organization.

The remaining chapters will pinpoint the six cardinal functions to bear in mind to apply human relations in personal leadership. A separate chapter will be devoted to each of these functions, with a bonus chapter on conducting "group thinks."

Now let's turn to a worker's-eye view of the boss.

2 *A worker's-eye view of what makes a good boss*

How much room is there for improvement in first-line leadership? For some answers, we'll look at a few scoreboards to see how workers feel about their immediate bosses. Top-level executives are often in the dark about this, because the first-line leaders tend to pass only good news upward.

We will find that workers have strong convictions about what they expect of a boss. When the boss comes up to these expectations, production and morale usually improve. When the expectations are short-circuited, there is often a cold war—worker indifference, dissatisfaction, and subtle opposition.

What management wants from first-line bosses jibes only partly with what the workers want. There is about a fifty-fifty chance that employees and top executives will agree that a particular foreman is a good leader (42, 128).

The firms represented in the following cases are mostly large, wealthy, and leaders in their fields. The records we shall look into, which both compliment and censure the firms, show their shoulder-to-shoulder leadership to be spotty. Leadership may be effective in one section, but at low ebb in the adjoining section which does similar work. Such ups and downs within a firm suggest that its leadership has been on a catch-

19

as-catch-can, or inspirational, basis, rather than on the solid base of operationally tested methods.

From the cases we will review, some points will emerge which will explain why some leaders have cooperative followers, while others seem to be pushing against a stone wall.

Do bosses have to be disliked?

Does the job of bossing require the boss to do things which will make him disliked by his workers? The records indicate that it depends upon the way the boss goes about his job. As an example, here is a capsule summary of research findings reported from the Institute for Social Research, at Ann Arbor, by Dr. Nathan Maccoby, who is now director of the division of research of the School of Public Relations and Communications, at Boston University (79).

	Strong liking for boss	Moderate liking for boss	Neutral or dislike
Percentage of railroad laborers (men)	38	49	12
Percentage of office clerks (girls) ..	42	32	25

Those bosses were all experienced. The workers were semi-skilled.

These, and other records, indicate that bosses are not as widely disliked as some critics imagine. And also that bosses are not followed as enthusiastically as some would hope. There are bosses and bosses. The degree of liking for a boss depends partly upon the boss's general personality and partly on his bossing methods. But there are some other influences which come from the working situation, as we shall see in a few pages.

The leader's main job is not winning a popularity contest, though there is some relationship between the workers' liking for him and the amount of work they turn out. This relationship is not uniform; it depends upon several other factors (115).

In the case of the railroad laborers, the gangs who liked their bosses the most generally produced the most work. But with the office clerks, there was no significant difference in productivity under bosses who were liked or disliked. Records from other industries and other types of work suggest that in general there is a little higher output when the boss is liked. This is easy to understand, because a boss who is liked is not likely to be arousing hostility or anxiety among his followers.

In addition, actions which might be considered objectionable when done by a boss who is disliked are often accepted as O.K. when done by one who is liked (46, 47).

Notice that a larger share of the office clerks gave their bosses the short end of the measuring stick. This may reflect differences in the office and railroad situations. The office work was routine processing for a multibillion-dollar firm; the clerks had practically no variety in their work. But the railroad gangs had an assortment of tasks which gave them variety in their work. The work situation is usually more satisfying when the workers do a variety of operations that are within their abilities (94, 126).

The office clerks were much younger than the railroaders, and also had several years more schooling. It is probable that youthfulness and more education inclined the clerks toward higher expectations about their jobs. When these higher expectations were not realized, there was some anxiety which could put their leaders in a less favorable light (83).

Undercover leaders

When a crew has a general dislike for the boss as a person, the situation is ripening for them to look upon a fellow worker as the real leader. When there is such an undercover leader, the official boss sometimes becomes a record keeper and errand boy for the worker whom the group prefers to follow. It seems surprising, but in such circumstances production and morale are often helped, provided the nominal boss takes his role as chief clerk gracefully. The workers rally around the person who comes up to what they expect from a leader, and he may not always be the one who is designated by the higher-ups as the leader. Throughout most of the cases reported, you will notice the recurrence of the importance of the leader meeting certain expectations which his followers have.

Some firms try to prevent undercover leaders popping up by teaming up the designated leaders in pairs. One member of the pair is chosen as the technical expert, or taskmaster. The other member is selected for his personal qualities and his skill as a smoother-outer to patch up the ruffled feelings (anxiety and hostility) his partner arouses.

Such smoothing out is sometimes the main task of the assistant foreman, or assistant to the executive. Sometimes, patching up things makes a private secretary worth her weight in uranium. There is a danger, however, in an organizational setup where one person is appointed to repair the human-relations damage done by a taskmaster. The technical man may become careless about his human relations and develop into a liability beyond the patching-up stage.

*They turned out more work for the bosses they thought
used better human-relations methods*

Should we take much stock in what workers say about
their boss's leadership abilities? This chartoon deals primarily
with the human-relations methods of bosses, as sized up by
their workers. The boss's likeableness as a person is not included. The records are about the bosses in 14 office departments of a Kentucky plant of a large corporation. The findings were reported by Dr. Charles W. Lawshe, of the Occupational Research Center at Purdue University (70).

At once, these office workers found it easy to tell what
they looked upon as strong and as weak points in their bosses.
The employees also agreed fairly consistently with each other
in sizing up their bosses' skills in human relations. The leader
wasn't the only one who could do some sizing up.

Some of the bosses' human-relations ways were pictured
by the workers as:

Being easy to see to talk over a problem.
Not criticizing for things that couldn't be helped.
Being prompt in taking care of complaints.
Making good on promises to the workers.
Showing an interest in the employee's suggestions.
Giving good explanations of how to avoid errors.
Giving sincere answers, and no run-around or stalling.
Discussing why work changes may be necessary.
Giving an employee recognition for good work.
Informing workers about what is going on, or contemplated.

You can easily analyze how each of those ways would keep
from increasing hostility or anxiety in the workers.

The production of each department was evaluated by six of the plant's top executives. Among other factors considered

They turned out more work for the bosses they thought were good

Productivity in bosses' departments:

59

43

Workers LEAST favorable to bosses

Workers MOST favorable to bosses

in productivity were: How much trouble the work group caused; how it could handle a rush job; how efficiently it could produce the answers when needed.

The columns in this chartoon represent that overall productivity index. The seven departments whose workers perceived their bosses as weakest in human relations are on the left. Their productivity averaged significantly below the other departments. In fact, six out of these seven departments produced below the lowest of the departments where the bosses were sized up more favorably by the workers.

Apparently these workers knew a good boss when they worked under one who came up to their expectations.

How the bosses sized up themselves

Did the boss have an accurate idea of how his methods stacked up with his workers' expectations? Dr. Lawshe found that it depended upon the boss. The bosses who were most aware of how their workers sized them up were usually the bosses who won the most favorable reports.

On the other hand, the bosses who were weakest in human relations came farthest from the mark in knowing where they stood with their work forces. This suggests that lacking sensitivity to what workers expected from them was one element in keeping these bosses at the bottom of the heap. These bosses led as they wanted to, not as the workers wanted to be led.

Another case of 685 workers in a public-utility office department revealed that slightly more than half of the employees looked upon their bosses as average to poor in handling people (87).

A few companies now get the rank and file to size up a fellow worker who is being judged for promotion to leadership. The followers thus help select their bosses, and they may give thumbs up to those who are most aware of the way workers want to be handled.

As far as that goes, a large proportion of workers have always picked their bosses when employment was plentiful. If a boss didn't come up to their expectations, they quit and got a job under another boss.

These telephone crews traded bosses

Do different crews doing similar work want about the same leadership qualities from their bosses? If there is a consensus among workers about what they expect from a boss, it will give practical targets for training leaders for a particular type of organization.

This question was tested with telephone-installation crews in a large city. The experiment was made by Dr. Jay M. Jackson, as part of the human-relations program at McGill University. It was financed by the Defence Research Board of Canada, and was facilitated by the cooperation of the company and the labor union involved (51).

These installers worked in nine-man crews. There were clear lines of authority and communication in the company; the workers understood these from long experience with official channels. The supervisors had not been given leadership training; this analysis was a preliminary step in working out a training plan.

The test was simple. Foremen who had been sized up as superior by their own crews switched jobs with other foremen whose crews had reported them as below average. Would the foremen sized up as poor by one crew also be considered poor by their new crew?

Four months after the switch, the leadership qualities of the same supervisors were again sized up by their new crews. The foremen who had been rated good by their original crews came out with almost the same score with their new crews. And the men originally judged as poor were still judged as equally poor by the new crews.

Qualities they expected the boss to have

The crews apparently had unwritten standards about what they expected from their leaders. Switching leaders did not change these expectations. A new foreman with a different personality did not cause a shift in the crews' underlying wishes about how their leader should perform.

One of the crews broke out in open rebellion under their new boss. This crew had been accustomed to an exceptionally able boss who came well up to their expectations. But the replacement they got in the switch was far below their expectations, and the crew showed strong hostility toward the higher management for making the switch. Apparently caution is needed when a boss the workers have thought was "their kind of boss" is taken away from them.

These crews of linemen expected the following, among other things, of their leaders:

Up to expectations	Below expectations
To listen sympathetically to complaints and give assurance he will do something to remove the causes.	To be told off when a complaint is made to the boss.
To speak about mistakes in private, and try to help the worker who made them.	To be bawled out, or humiliated in front of others.

Up to expectations	Below expectations
When a rule has been broken, to explain the seriousness, give fair warning, and try to understand the worker's side of the story.	To be bullied into behaving better, or be threatened with discipline.
Boss fully in touch with rules, and interprets them in the best interests of his men.	Sticks to rules when it suits his interests, but not when it does not suit his interests.
When worker is puzzled about a job, the boss tries to understand the reason and set him straight.	To be told it's no concern of the boss that you can't understand, and to work it out for yourself.
Worker feels perfectly free to air a grievance to boss.	Workers feel they don't dare air it to the boss.
Boss considers each man on his merits when designating men for special courses or other advantages.	Boss favoring a certain few he considers his friends.
To put the interests of the crew members first when dealing with higher-ups.	When boss shows he rates keeping in good with higher-ups above the interests of the men.
To take a real personal interest in the men on his crew.	To take practically no personal interest in the men under him.

It should be easy for you by now to trace the thread of hostility or anxiety that runs through each of those expectations.

The boss as an unmentioned factor in labor trouble

One crew of the linemen went into rebellion when they got a poor boss in the switch. When bosses do not come up to workers' expectations, is this likely to cause tension which may spill over and motivate the workers to go on a strike?

The underlying motives in a strike situation were measured by Dr. John James at a West Coast port city. One establishment was in the midst of a strike. The strikers were talked

More of the strikers wished their bosses were better

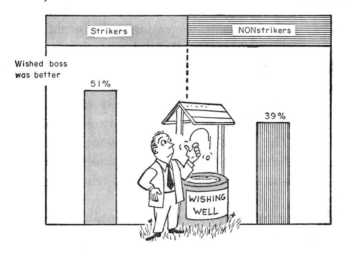

to individually in the union hall, to find out the strength of their feelings toward certain job factors that might have precipitated the trouble (53).

As a base for comparison, the same attitudes were determined in nonstriking employees of a similar organization in the same locality.

A much larger proportion of the strikers were dissatisfied with their interactions with their bosses, as this chartoon pictures. The strikers also felt that their bosses needed improvement more than the nonstrikers did.

The strikers had griped about this a little longer than the nonstrikers had. The strikers were also a little less certain of any improvement ever coming about in their bosses. And they thought it would take considerably longer before the ugly duckling bosses would improve.

Why didn't the strikers come right out and include better relations with the bosses in their demands?

Because the strikers felt they had more control over such factors as: seniority rights, wages, interesting qualities of their jobs, working conditions, work week, and the chance to get ahead, in the order listed. They felt most hopeless about doing anything to get a better boss.

So the strike had been called, naturally enough, on issues over which they felt they had most control—seniority rights and wages. The bosses' methods were not specifically mentioned. But the attitude records indicate strongly that this dissatisfaction with the bosses was a potent motivating factor in the hassle.

This is an example of how a gripe (hostility) can spill over and spread to related things which are not the primary causes. A simple example is the worker who is bawled out on the job, so punishes his children when he gets home (73).

Six aspects of dissatisfactions which become motives

Hidden reasons, of which people may not be aware themselves, often motivate behavior which is puzzling to outsiders. An example of this is the way hostility toward a boss who does not come up to expectations can be a background cause of industrial strife. Strikes are rarely called directly because of the boss. But when the boss is not up to snuff in human relations, then the group may go to bat to win gains in sectors where they are more hopeful of getting some results.

The force of motives from such dissatisfactions is considered owing to six aspects of the dissatisfactions (64):

1. Amount of dissatisfaction	"How satisfied are you with the way your boss treats you and handles his work?"
2. Strength of that feeling	"How strongly do you feel that you want your boss to be better?"
3. Time before improvement is expected	"How soon do you expect your boss will become better?"
4. Personal power to bring about the change	"How much control do you think you have in getting the kind of boss you want?"
5. How long desire has existed	"How long have you felt this way about wanting the improvement in your boss?"
6. Certainty about realizing the desire	"Assuming that you do your best work, how certain are you that your boss will improve?"

In this West Coast case, the strikers were a little stronger motivated than the nonstrikers on all six aspects. The last two —length of desire, and certainty—were found to be the least significant.

Would granting a wage increase and making seniority changes prevent a recurrence of trouble in such a situation?

And why were the office workers in these firms not as dissatisfied with their bosses? Can it be because white-collar workers have better bosses? Or are they easier to satisfy with a mediocre boss?

Do white-collar bosses get more favorable reports?

The first report in this chapter compared office workers' and railroad laborers' liking for their bosses. The office workers were girls living in a big city. The railroad workers were older men, from small towns, working in the open country. We saw how liking for the boss could be influenced by sex, age, work variety, education, and small-town or big-city conditions.

Now for a story that does not deal with general liking, but with some specific human-relations methods of the bosses. These records are of men only, and of workers in the same big-city electric-power company. This summary shows how 1,792 white-collar office men described their bosses, compared with the way 4,785 blue-collar men in the same firm described their bosses. These records are from the files of the Survey Research Center (60).

Human-relations method	Per cent of white-collar bosses	Per cent of blue-collar bosses
"My boss makes a real effort to place people in their best jobs"	52	39
"Boss stands up for me"	72	58
"He is reasonable in what he expects from me"	78	65
"He takes an interest in me and understands my problems"	65	54
"He gives recognition for good work" ...	74	62
"My boss gives me help when I really need it"	80	72

The reports on the white-collar bosses were distinctly more favorable on those counts. Records from other firms indicate that the white-collar bosses usually get the top records on such details. These differences throw some light on why it is difficult to form a union of white-collar workers. But this does not mean that every white-collar boss is the sort the clerks would rescue first from a sinking ship.

It is possible that white-collar bosses get more favorable reports than they merit. White-collar work usually enjoys greater social prestige, even when the pay is lower, than blue-collar jobs. Satisfaction from this prestige may spill over and motivate the office workers to feel that other things about their jobs are rosy. Some of this rosiness may give the boss a brighter halo than he deserves.

Blue-collar anxiety about job prestige

There is another side of this social force of prestige. Blue-collar workers are likely to have some unspoken anxiety about their jobs, because their work is not regarded as high class.

This blue-collar dissatisfaction about job prestige may spill over, too, to color the workers' interactions with the boss, and to tarnish the halo they give him. Then the boss becomes the butt of defensive attitudes which really spring from the public's small esteem for the category of work. If the blue-collar worker can't go up in the world, then he may try to chisel his boss down to size.

In view of this, it may be that the blue-collar boss needs better leadership skills than do many white-collar bosses. Upgrading the prestige of a job may make the leadership more effective (66, Chapter 12).

There was only one respect in which the blue-collar workers in this large utility firm had the more favorable picture of their bosses. Slightly more of the blue-collar men were satisfied with the responsibility given them in their work than white-collar men. This might have been because they were less ambitious. But it was a fact that the blue-collar work did provide a greater variety of operations for each worker. Job simplification had been used extensively in the offices, in contrast, so the white-collar work was highly routinized.

Some time later this firm tried out a program of enlarging some of the office jobs which had been simplified previously. This job enlarging gave the office clerks more responsibility and variety of operations. J. D. Elliott reports that it was found to increase output (29).

These navy squads indicate that the leader should "feel his way"

It begins to appear that the leader's job will vary, depending partly upon the makeup and expectations of the group he is leading. City office women may expect different things from their leaders than do small-town men.

The leader's tasks also depend upon the type of work his crew is doing at the moment—this even when he is leading the same people, at the same rate of pay. When a crew changes from one type of work to another, there is often a shift in the mental and social forces in their interactions. Leadership methods which are high quality in one situation may turn out to be mediocre, or poor, in a different situation.

Dr. Launor Carter and colleagues have demonstrated this shift of forces when the crew changes from assembly to conference work. This was a laboratory-type study, made for the Office of Naval Research (19).

The interactions between the men were observed while they were at work. Eight naval cadets worked together in each group observed. No one else was in the room. Their interactions were watched through a one-way glass, and their voices were picked up by microphones.

These crews had only slight acquaintance with each other at the start; they were not especially cohesive crews. Each man had previously been observed in other groups. For these final test squads, the cadets were grouped so that all the men on a squad had about equal leadership potential. They worked without an assigned leader. These so-called leaderless groups made it possible to observe the spontaneous interactions while engaged in different kinds of work.

Assembling bridges and observation stands was one kind of work they were given to do. An equal amount of time was spent in conference work. Both types of work required the men to work together in solving problems; the assembly work dealt with tangible problems, the conference work with ideas and feelings. The crucial difference was the goal toward which they were headed—complete an assembly, or reach a decision in the conference session.

The bars in the chartoon show the differences in the men's interactions, depending upon the tasks they were working at.

When the construction was their goal, the most frequent interaction was as followers, or workers. For example: they imitated others, asked questions, helped others. This type of interaction was almost missing when the same men were "in conference" in the same room and at the same rate of pay.

When reaching a group decision in conference was their goal, shown by the right-hand portions of the bars, their chief interaction was starting action. Examples: they proposed

Different interactions in construction work than in conferences

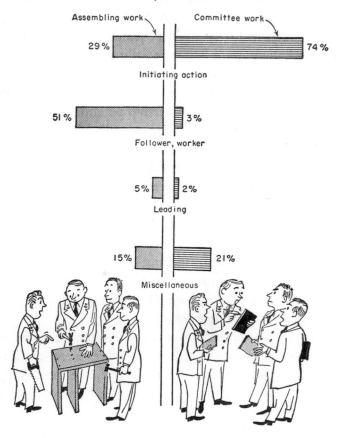

courses of action, asked the other fellow for his opinion, asked for information, agreed with others.

Arguing (included in miscellaneous) accounted for 10 per cent of the conference interactions, but for only 2 per cent while on the construction work. A conference leader may have greater need to "pour oil on troubled waters."

In another phase of the same experiments, work squads of four men were compared with squads of eight men. It was found that doubling the size of the groups changed the inter-actions between members while at work.

The larger crews had a greater share of friendly inter-actions and giving information. Expressing opinions and argu-ing also increased. But there was less question asking, less action as a follower, and less agreeing.

Apparently the leader should be a "feeler," who feels his way and adapts his methods to changes in the size of the group as well as to the job goals of the group.

The size of group being led made a difference

Here is some additional material about the size of the group being led. The "practical-experience route" of leadership training has been to start a new man handling a small group, then work him up to leading larger crews. But there are now strong indications that success in leading a small group may not carry over to help out with a larger group—unless the leader is a feeler who can adapt his methods to the demands of the group.

Actual operating groups have been analyzed to find how different the demands are upon leaders under various condi-tions. A wide range of face-to-face groups were included:

business and industrial, social, military, community, and athletic.

The groups, and their leaders, were reported on by actual members, who ranged from young adults to elderly people.

More was expected of the leaders of the large groups

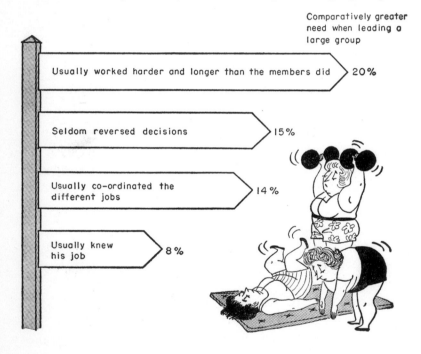

Comparatively **greater** need when leading **a** large group

Usually worked harder and longer than the members did > 20%

Seldom reversed decisions > 15%

Usually co-ordinated the different jobs > 14%

Usually knew his job > 8%

The leader was considered good or excellent for 365 of these groups. This chartoon deals with these 365 top-quality leaders. Of these top leaders, 184 led groups of more than 30 members per group. The other 181 had groups smaller than this to lead. A comparison of these successful leaders of the large and of the smaller groups was made by Dr. John K.

Hemphill, who is now a consultant for the U.S. Air Force (45).

These leaders were contrasted on 70 methods or procedures they used in leading their groups. It was found that the size of the group made a real difference in the usefulness of 47 out of the 70 methods. The probabilities are better than 95 out of 100 that these 47 differences were not due to chance, with these groups.

The larger groups were found in general to demand much more of their leaders, if the leaders were to be successful. Leading a large group may require a different kind of leadership, rather than just more of the same methods that work well with smaller groups.

The 47 very real differences can be lumped into two broad classes. The one class is highlighted in this chartoon. It reflects a greater demand for strength, reliability, predictability, and even moral or physical courage in leading a larger group. Situations calling for these characteristics apparently are less likely to arise in a small group.

The other class shows that the leader of large groups has more need to be firm and impersonal. For example: he was seldom lax with members, never allowed exceptions to the rules, seldom explained why he did things, listened less to others, had less consideration for individual members.

These findings also indicate that the larger groups inclined to be leader-centered, while the smaller groups functioned better if they were led in a member-centered fashion. A large group may tolerate restrictive methods which would throw a smaller group into revolt.

Such findings help us understand why the successful leader of a small crew may be a washout when promoted to division head. Or why the dynamic vice-president may do more harm than good when he tries to "sell" a pet notion to a small round-table meeting.

Such records remind us again that the leader's methods may need to be tailored to the needs of the particular group he is facing—or shoulder-to-shoulder with—at the moment. Trying to use the same cookbook methods in every situation can lower the quality of leadership in many instances. There are times to be leader-centered, times to use member-centered methods. Times to be permissive, times to be restrictive. Times for democratic methods, while other times and situations may call for autocratic methods if the group is to make headway toward its goals.

A large share of leaders didn't lead

Considering everything, how large a share of our leaders in everyday affairs can be ranked as successful?

Making a profit for the business or club may not always tell the story. That may overlook interactions in human relations which will make it more difficult to earn a profit in future years. For the summing-up chartoon in this chapter we will not look at company ledgers, but will get the verdict from the people who are presumably being led. As some firms remind their executives, it takes followers to make a leader.

In Dr. Hemphill's analysis of the leadership of 500 ongoing groups, the members reported on the effectiveness of their presumed leaders. Both men and women followers—members, workers, etc.—were included; their average age was thirty years (44).

There were 135 of the leaders who ranged from only fair

to downright bad as leaders. This comes to 27 per cent who did not pan out in their followers' eyes.

Some of the overall results of the mixture of good and poor leadership are reflected in this chartoon. This covers all 500 groups, totaling some 15,000 followers.

Most of the groups did not lean heavily on their leaders

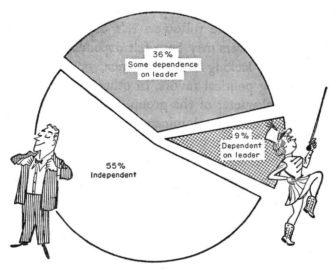

This chartoon reveals that the majority were followers in name only. Most of them felt they were acting on their own individual responsibility, and felt practically no dependence upon their nominal leader. This majority leaned more heavily on themselves, and on other members (undercover leaders), than on their designated leaders. They would not mind taking a day off from work to go fishing, even when the boss was driving to cut down absenteeism.

If these figures represent conditions across the country (and they are the widest sample available), they imply that fully half the leaders have little influence their followers can detect. This becomes more significant when we recall that the successful leaders are included in this chartoon. A proportion of the leaders who were considered successful may have been liked well enough personally, but they were not using methods that caused the followers to lean on them.

The smallest cut of the pie represents the one-out-of-eleven leaders upon whom the followers felt dependent. Some of these faithful followers may have felt dependent for personal reasons, such as lacking self-confidence, or being clinging vines, or seeking political favors. In other instances, it could be due to the character of the group, as in a religious assemblage organized around a dominant leader.

The dependent 9 per cent would be expected to be most responsive to paternalism in the leader's methods. Fringe benefits, for example, would be expected to be more satisfying to that minority. But to the independent majority, the benefits might be something they hoped to get more of, and not something to motivate them, say, to be more faithful in attendance at work, or to produce more per hour.

*   *   *

The capsule reports given thus far begin to give an outline sketch of what it takes to be an effective leader in our times. This picture is not the same as used to be drawn by tycoons when they gave advice to aspiring leaders. Perhaps the times have changed the demands of what is expected from leaders today. At any rate, it is now being found that the leader has to work through psychological and social forces—prestige, interactions, hostility, anxiety—not with plausible platitudes.

Many of the old maxims about leadership are dead horses that are slow to lie down.

In the following chapter we shall fill in more details of this picture by comparing the results of two general styles of leadership methods. What effects do the democratic style and the autocratic style have on production and morale?

3 *Styles of leadership, and the climates they create*

It seems to take all kinds of leaders to keep the world going. And each kind of leader seems to create a human climate which has specific effects on his followers.

Although the number of different methods used by leaders must be enormous, it has been found easy to classify most as representing one or another style of leadership. The classification which has been most used is:

Autocratic style   *In contrast with*   Democratic style

There are more recently named styles, which partly overlap the democratic and autocratic. Although these create about the same climates as the democratic or autocratic, each does emphasize some variation which has practical significance:

Authoritarian	*In contrast*	Equalitarian
Dictatorial	*with*	Facilitative
Leader-centered		Group-centered
Production-centered		Worker-centered
Restrictive		Permissive

Everyday terms that are used to describe bosses can also be lined up in the same two columns:

44

High-pressure	*In contrast*	Low-pressure
Close supervision	*with*	General supervision
Tough		Tender
Watchdog		Bird dog

In this chapter we will look into records of production and morale, to see what difference these contrasting styles of leading may cause. In some situations one style seems to be more effective, in other situations the contrasted style.

First, we wonder which style of man is more likely to **try** to become a leader.

The self-elected leaders were bossier

Naval reserve officer corpsmen were used for this laboratory-type experiment made by Dr. Launor Carter for the Office of Naval Research. You may recall that the interactions of naval men, while working in squads of four persons, were watched through a one-way glass and listened to through a microphone pickup (18).

Each man in a squad appeared to have about equal leadership potential, based on his performance in previous squads.

For this critical test, some of the squads were set to work without a designated leader. In other groups, one member at random was appointed leader, and the other members were told he was the leader so there would be no misunderstanding about it.

But the squads which started out without a designated leader soon had leaders. One member invariably took charge of things on his own initiative. Some of these self-elected leaders simply wanted to run things. Others of the self-elected tried to stampede the squad into accepting their ideas.

The members quickly perceived that these "natural" leaders wanted to run them, and their interactions became greatly

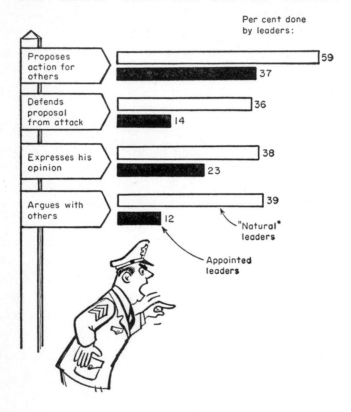

The "natural" leaders used autocratic methods

Per cent done
by leaders:

Proposes action for others	59 / 37
Defends proposal from attack	36 / 14
Expresses his opinion	38 / 23
Argues with others	39 / 12

"Natural" leaders

Appointed leaders

changed. Apparently a person touches off different reactions
in others when he is leading than when he is just "one of
the crew."

Some of the significant differences in the ways the two
kinds of leaders handled the crews are shown in this chartoon.

These differences were observed when the squads were working in conference sessions, or "group thinks."

The upper bar in each pair depicts the "natural" leaders who pushed their way into taking charge of the squads. The lower bars are for the leaders who were appointed, whether they were eager for the jobs or not.

With four men of equal ability in a crew, it would be par for each man to initiate 25 per cent of the interactions if the group operated on a free and easy basis. The top pair of bars, however, show that both the self-elected and the appointed leaders did more than their 25 per cent share of proposing actions. But the self-elected leader did more than twice his fair share of telling the others in the squad what to do: bossiness.

The contrasts between the other pairs of bars indicate that the self-elected and the appointed-at-random leaders used much different styles in their interactions with other crew members. They produced different climates. The men who itched to lead the others went about it in a much different style than those who had leadership thrust upon them.

Are business leaders on the bossy side?

How does this work out in business? Small conference groups who were working on sales methods, safety programs, and other business problems, have been analyzed by Dr. Irving J. Lee. Out of the 143 leaders studied in such business conferences, 53 per cent clearly inclined toward autocratic or bossy methods in handling the conferences. This may reflect a tendency for the self-elected style of leader to be the one who was more likely to rise to business leadership in the past (72).

Other researches have revealed that the person who inclined toward bossiness could not see much difference between these two styles of leading. This implies that the autocrat's human relations may be poor without his realizing it (56).

How many people in the general population incline toward the autocratic side, how many toward the democratic when they follow their natural impulses in leading others? We recall that there is what is known as a normal distribution of human qualities in the general population. Most of us are not at one extreme or the other in any human quality, but somewhere between the extremes, whatever the extremes happen to be (65).

Thus in a random selection of people, about one-fourth would be autocratic, about one-fourth democratic, and the remaining one-half in the so-called average range.

Check that against Dr. Lee's observations of 53 per cent of the men conducting business conferences who were plainly on the autocratic side. Those conference leaders had twice the normal expectancy of the autocratic style.

Usually the democratic methods get better results

In routine office work, as well as in conferences, the style of the leader has been found to influence the interactions of the work group. These differences add up and affect production in some kinds of work, but not in all kinds of work situations. Another illustration of the desirability of the leadership methods being fitted to the expectations and needs of the particular group being led.

This chartoon shows some of the findings with routine office workers in an eleven-billion-dollar corporation. Most of the clerks were unmarried girls, high-school graduates, and

The higher producing offices had the democratic bosses

Bosses who used democratic methods:

100%

34%

High-output offices   Lower-output offices

OUR NEW PLAN

an average of twenty-five years old. The analysis charted was made by Dr. Daniel Katz and staff of the Survey Research Center (58).

The left column reveals that all the bosses of the high-producing offices used a democratic style of leading. They talked things over with the workers before deciding what should be done. These democratic bosses tried to win cooperation rather than act as the brain issuing orders. Few of them approved of the caste system of seating in the company dining rooms. Their methods and attitudes produced a climate which made it easier for employees to work without feeling humiliation or resentment—less arousing of hostility or anxiety.

The clerks in this democratic atmosphere shared final common goals in their work. When one clerk caught up on her batch of work, she turned to help another. That mutual help boosted the overall output.

That stubby column on the right tells a different story for the 12 low-producing offices. Only one-third of their supervisors were of the democratic style. The bosses in most of these low-output offices set up autocratic climates which apparently cut into productivity. These autocratic bosses were inclined to give orders bluntly, supervise closely—"breathe down our necks"—enforce rules strictly, drive for more production, and do the planning themselves. Their workers were given tasks to do, rather than commonly shared goals.

The leader who drives in autocratic ways for more output has been found, in most instances, to keep a vicious cycle going. The harder these bosses pushed for production, the more unfavorable the climate became. That lowered production a little, so they put on still more pressure, which in turn ushered in another cold front and dropped production a bit further.

In some situations the autocratic methods worked better

But with some of the least-skilled workers in this same company, it was a different story. In the case of the least-skilled crews, the autocratic style got a little better production. How come?

It is thought that some workers, who have had years of autocratic commanding, have become so used to expecting to be pushed that that was the only way left to get output out of them. When put under a democratic boss, they became bewildered (anxiety?), and were unable to depend upon their own initiative.

Semiskilled railroad laborers illustrate another situation where a democratic gang climate was not the more productive. The members of these gangs were married men, averaging forty years old, and had not attended high school. They had had some twenty years' work experience on the average, in contrast with the office clerks who averaged less than five years' experience. The output of these railroaders was not related one way or the other to the climates set by their bosses (59).

Such examples highlight the probability that under present varied conditions there is not "one best style of leading." The style may need to be adapted to the aspirations, expectations, close-range goals, and past leadership experiences of the particular work group. The one universal requirement, or touchstone for leadership, may turn out to be flexibility—adapting methods to fit the needs of a definite situation.

The meaning of democratic leadership

The term, "democratic leadership," can easily be misleading. It is natural at first to think that it means wearing old clothes, eating bread and gravy, and being a regular guy who does not put on high-hat airs. As the phrase is used in human relations, however, it means leading in ways that give the followers *a feeling of taking part in setting the goals and methods of their groups.* It is not doing nothing, but coordinating and unleashing the best human forces for a group activity (76).

Permissive vs. restrictive leadership in a government operation

Now for an example of the contrasts between permissive and restrictive styles of leading. We will lift the lid on a Federal establishment for this example. The employees were professional and technical people, doing highly skilled work. The two divisions compared had the same regulations, pay scales, and red tape. Their work was parallel. The main difference was the style of their supervisors.

One division was under a strict boss who kept close watch to see that all the small type in the rule book was followed—a restrictive style of bossing. The chief of the parallel section allowed the employees some leeway: they watched the red tape for themselves, permissive style.

The work in both divisions required similar contacts with others within the division. There could be no avoiding these interactions. How satisfied were the employees with these prescribed contacts? And did the climates set by the division chiefs affect these work relations? Those questions were answered by records gathered by Dr. Robert Tannenbaum and staff members of the Institute of Industrial Relations of the University of California, in Los Angeles (88).

The difference between the columns in this chartoon shows that the people under the restrictive boss were more likely to reject the people they had to contact (hostility). The restrictive climate which was set by the chief apparently made the human relations throughout his entire division much less satisfying to the workers.

More satisfying relationships on the job when the boss was permissive

Degree of worker
satisfaction with
contacts on the
job:

62

50

Restrictive
supervision

Permissive
supervision

This greater rejection of fellow employees carried over to after-work hours. Evening and weekend socializing with others from the division was less frequent among the workers with the restrictive boss.

But the workers under the permissive, or more democratic chief, were much more satisfied with their jobs. They also had higher morale (less anxiety).

Studies of other groups would lead us to expect more grapevine rumors in the restrictive division. And more cliques. Gossip and cliques have been found to flourish best in a restrictive climate (1, 2, 32).

The hostility and anxiety triggered by a restrictive atmosphere appears to run over. The bad feelings often become directed against innocent bystanders who wonder what makes people treat them that way. Poor human relations that start at work commonly spill over to cause poor human relations off the job.

In this Federal installation, the workers under the permissive leader felt that their production was better than average. Those under the restrictive chief felt their production was not up to snuff. And to complicate this aspect, the bigger chiefs, 3,000 miles away in Washington, thought the restrictive boss had the more productive division. Washington was more favorably impressed when the red tape they promulgated was visibly enforced.

The increase in the size of private as well as public establishments probably results in a beefing up of rules, regulations, and standard procedures. This condition would put the first-line leaders under pressure to lean in the restrictive, or autocratic direction—watchdogs of the rules, regardless of their natural preferences.

Because big-scale operations gravitate into a bureaucratic system of rules and controls, as restrictive as the income tax blanks, the big outfit may have especial need to encourage a permissive climate whenever it is possible.

Worker-centered vs. production-centered leadership

What is the difference in human climate under a worker-centered leader and under a production-centered leader?

When an employee is absent from work, the worker-centered boss is concerned about possible illness or accident to the worker. But the production-centered boss would be more concerned about the department's getting behind schedule because of the absence. A large share of the attitudes and decisions of a leader can be classified as centering either on production itself, or on the workers behind the production.

Among the parallel offices at headquarters of a large company, 37 per cent of the first-line bosses were clearly worker centered. They tended to emphasize the human-relations aspects of their work.

There were 35 per cent who were production centered, stressing the technical aspects of the work. They did not show much interest in the clerks as people.

The remainder of the supervisors were not clearly in either of these classes, and were not classified.

The upper bar in the chartoon shows that in the high-producing offices, almost all of the classifiable bosses were worker centered. In the low-output offices, scarcely one-third were classifiable as worker centered (58).

In the case of blue-collar railroad workers, much the same relationship has been uncovered. The high-producing gangs felt that their foreman showed more personal interest in the workers, especially in their families and similar off-the-job problems. This tendency was not as marked as with the white-collar workers charted here, but was still meaningful (59).

Why is production helped when the boss focuses more on the worker than on the details of the work? The "parental attitudes" of the worker-centered leader seemed to motivate the employees to work harder. Less anxiety was aroused to

Bosses who were worker-centered had higher-producing work groups

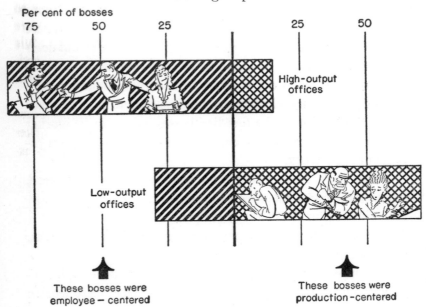

Per cent of bosses
75   50   25   25   50

High-output offices

Low-output offices

↑ These bosses were employee – centered

↑ These bosses were production-centered

upset them or block their efforts. The climate encouraged the feeling among the office clerks that they were more than cogs in a big machine, and this spirit apparently increased their aspirations to get more things done.

Contrary to what we might expect, the worker-centered bosses did not have as good a gain in morale as in production. Among the office clerks charted, for example, morale was determined by their satisfactions with pay, status of their jobs (prestige), and the company in general.

The workers in the high-morale offices reported that their bosses took only a little more interest in them as people. But this difference between high- and low-morale offices was not overwhelming. It was enough to mean a little something, but not significant as to productivity (94).

Contrary to what we may at first believe, this is looked upon as owing to the higher personal aspirations which workers seemed to get in a worker-centered climate. As individual goals were set higher, the clerks produced more, in hope of winning higher status of some sort. Their work climate gave them more ambition, which touched off hopes which could not always be fulfilled. Ambitions not reached touch off anxiety.

When top management laments about the workers' lack of ambition or initiative, management may be revealing a great deal about the human climate in the work place.

Whether an office has a worker-centered climate or not depends to an extent upon the style of the higher-up bosses. When the bigger boss shows personal interest in his first-line bosses, these in turn usually show more personal interest in their workers—another example of the endless chain of inter-actions. The style of the big boss is telegraphed all down the chain of command. Grownups, as well as children, pick up the characteristics and attitudes of those whom they feel have more power (77, 85).

Absenteeism was related to the style of leadership in this power company

Absence from work to go fishing provides an example of some of the end results of the human climate of a work place. This climate is an influence in shaping the final common goals of the work group—or causes the absence of work-motivating goals.

It has seemed logical to assume that absenteeism was due to irresponsibility on the part of some workers. In some instances, a high wage rate was thought to make some workers feel so rich that they could afford to take excessive time off. Employment interviewers have tried to size up applicants to pick the "steady-worker type."

But recent analyses of actual operating situations now point to human-relations factors as counting heavily in whether or not workers will be steady on the job. Blue-collar workers, who installed and maintained overhead lines for a large utility, provide a good example. The records were analyzed and reported by Drs. Floyd Mann and Howard Baumgartel (84).

The pay, equipment, duties, and other tangible arrangements were the same for all crews compared. But the crews were different in their absenteeism rates. Also, the human climates prevailing from crew to crew differed. These climates were presumably due partly, if not mostly, to the crews' immediate bosses. This summary indicates some of the significant ways in which the climates varied, as related to absenteeism:

How the men described the climate	Crews with FEWEST absences (per cent)	Crews with MOST absences (per cent)
"I feel I am really a part of the crew"	73	56
"Our foreman always, or usually, has time to talk over our personal problems"	67	43
"Our crew has lots of team spirit"	62	48
"Our crew is better than others at getting things done"	57	41
"I like my work a lot"	33	13
"My job gives me a good chance to do the things I can do best"	27	6
"Our foreman practically never has group discussions"	18	34

Let's look into each of those descriptions of the working climate, to put a finger on some of the methods of a style of leadership that produces lower absenteeism.

"I feel I am really a part of the crew" reflected the leadership objective of helping each worker to fit into and be accepted by the work group. The linemen who "felt they belonged" had less absenteeism.

"Our foreman has time to talk over our personal problems" indicated a worker-centered human-ness on the part of the boss. Those workers were more likely to have less anxiety, and to feel that they counted more as persons.

"Our crew has lots of team spirit" indicated the coordination of the members. Cohesiveness helped along by the human climate.

"I like my work a lot" hinged upon practically all of the leader's functions, including job placement.

"My job gives me a good chance to do the things I can do best" involved more than placement. It also reflected the leader's success in helping his men fit into the group, and coordinating the members. Also, there would be less anxiety when the worker was engaged at tasks in which he felt confident.

"Our foreman practically never has group discussions" was *negatively* related to absenteeism. The crews with group discussions did less playing hooky from work. The discussions on job problems stimulated the linemen to become more actively involved in the job; inspired them to work for group goals, and to have interest in the job as well as in fishing.

All in all, the climate which made some of the crews steadier workers was one that gave them an opportunity to take part in setting work goals and plans, and which acknowledged the dignity of each individual worker. The climate helped them feel they were making headway toward goals they had helped set, and toward which the chief was helping them make headway. Result: steadier workers.

Notice, in addition, that the climate which produced steadier workers gave them more satisfying interactions with fellow workers, and caused less triggering of hostility or anxiety. There was less social distance, and more cohesion, or pulling toward each other. Their relations were as enjoyable on the job as on fishing excursions.

The old-fashioned way to attack absenteeism was to put on a drive. Pressure was applied; perhaps rewards for steady attendance, penalties for skipping a day. It is now apparent that such drives do not change the climate in a direction to motivate a long-run gain in attendance. When reliance has been placed on such drives, absenteeism has usually become a problem again shortly after the drive was over. So, one drive has had to be followed by another.

The human climate in bargaining conferences

Another commonplace example of the power of human climate in leadership comes from bargaining sessions. In such conferences the climate is likely to be strained even before the interactions begin around the bargaining table. But in spite of that preliminary handicap, bargaining discussions vary greatly in their starting climates. It has been observed that the climate during the opening half hour is related to the progress—or lack of it—made during the session.

The chartoon tells the story about the climate during the first half hour of a session which laid an egg. It was between a truck drivers' union and representatives of employers. A Federal commissioner conducted the conference, which was observed by Dr. Wesley H. Osterberg, now a senior associate with Bruce Payne & Associates, management consultants (96).

One-third of the time charted was spent in miscellaneous talk, such as : "This meeting is to discuss a contract." "Average wage last year was 95 cents." "Somebody give me a match." These were neutral comments, which should do little to add or subtract hostility and anxiety from the atmosphere.

But nearly two-thirds of the time was spent on interactions which were primarily expressions of hostility. Expressions which could stir up a cold war. Both sides went in slugging with aggression, defense, and negation. This may have been intentional, on the old assumption that it catches the other side off balance. But what a slugging start usually does is throw the entire session off balance, as you have noticed in some congressional hearings (49).

Aggression took the biggest chunk of this slugging time, in the form of threats, criticism, insults, and belittling.

Defense took the next largest share of the slugging. The

The unsuccessful bargaining session got off on the wrong foot

Negation ½ minute
"We can't accept that!"

"Our proposal is fair!"

Miscellaneous
10 minutes
"Let's open
a window."

Questions
½ minute
"What is
the rate?"

Aggression
9½ minutes

"You'll be
sorry if
you try
that!"

Defense
8 minutes

Clarification
1½ minutes
"Let's say it
this way."

defense was mostly repetition of a previous statement, with no new facts added. While the defense may have been uttered in a friendly tone, it was a standing pat which could not clear the atmosphere. For the time being, a defensive comment would block progress toward the common goal, which was to reach an agreement and get the mess over with.

Only small slivers of the time were spent in interactions

which might dispel the cold front and make some headway toward an agreement. A half minute was devoted to a question. Questions to get information, or the viewpoint of the other side, have been found to improve the climate and help settle the issues. Clarification, which was also neglected at this session, works out in much the same way as questions in helping the climate.

For the 11 sessions that failed, the bulk of time at the bargaining table was spent in aggression, defense, and negation.

The successful sessions, on the other hand, were dominated by questions, clarification, and tossing the problem to the other side of the table: "Give me some ideas about how I can solve this problem."

The climate pictured in this chartoon can be compared with the average for 22 other groups who discussed equally serious topics, but topics on which they were not divided into two camps before sitting down to talk. Here is what was found by Dr. Robert F. Bales, of the Harvard Laboratory for Social Relations, in collaboration with Dr. Fred L. Strodtbeck, who is now with the University of Chicago law school (8):

	Per cent
Expressing opinions (gives own feelings; asks for others) ..	35
Positive actions (agrees, laughs, gives help)	25
Getting bearings (asks questions, gives information)	25
Suggests (gives or asks for solutions)	7.5
Negative actions (argues, belittles, stubborn attitude)	7.5

Some conference leaders, to insure a better climate, detail one person to ask clarifying questions, or make wisecracks even, to relieve tension before hostility builds up to a high-octane level.

Where do workers get their work goals?

We are now in a position to fill in more details in the picture of a successful leader. We have found that what is needed by the leader varies somewhat with the type of group he is leading. He should match the expectations of his particular group of presumed followers; this requires a fairly accurate notion of what his followers expect, as well as what the higher-ups expect from him.

Although various groups do not agree in everything they expect from the leaders they willingly follow, there are some common threads which merit special emphasis. These common expectations can be summed up like this: People who work shoulder-to-shoulder want to feel:

1. That they are making headway
2. That they are headed toward some goal they understand and accept.

That goal is shared by most of the members of the work team. It may be a goal the company approves, such as keeping down scrap, or increasing output. But it may be a goal headed in the other direction, such as to hold down output to what the workers think is a "reasonable" level, or to make life miserable for the boss by appearing to misunderstand his instructions, or by spreading grapevine rumors.

Work teams hit upon their goals by slowly developing a general understanding—a consensus—among themselves. The leader may be left outside as the group arrives at some understanding about these goals about what is fit and right. These goals are seldom put into words. But they are almost always there after a group has been together a few days—invisible barriers, or invisible forces, depending upon the nature of the goal aimed at.

Which direction these self-developed group goals are headed depends to a large extent, in most work groups, upon the human climate in their work place. These climates affect the interactions through which they pick up a general understanding of the goals the group tacitly agrees upon. Recall how the linemen in some crews developed unspoken goals about being steady workers? In a restrictive climate, the tacit goals are likely to amount to a rejection of the goals the boss tries to hammer into them.

The successful leader operates by mobilizing the mental and social forces within his followers, and heading these forces toward some common goals. He uses methods which create a climate and interactions which make the followers' goals clearer and more personal, more constructive for everybody concerned. And the followers sense that their leader is helping them make headway to reach these goals. Those broad statements can be pinned down to definite operational procedures, as the closing sections of this and the remaining chapters will do.

The six cardinal functions of personal leadership

Let's check back for a moment to Dr. Hemphill's analysis of 500 present-day leaders, and the methods they used. He compared the 365 successful leaders with the 135 who were failures. The contrasts between successes and failures made it possible to spot the factors which were significant in making the difference in leadership results (44).

Making quick decisions, for instance, was not found to be a significant element. Quick thinking was not generally needed by the leaders, although it may be helpful when the

A composite picture of the methods of 365 successful leaders

group is large, or is informally organized. Most work groups are of the informally organized sort.

The factors which were found to be significant in making a leader a success can be catalogued into six principal functions. Each of these functions puts a spotlight on one of the objectives the leader could well keep in mind in his day-to-day procedures. These six spotlighted functions are all focused on mobilizing the mental and social forces in the group so that the followers are motivated to work together toward goals they understand and accept.

These cardinal functions of personal leadership are listed on the six sides of this chartoon. Function A was found the most significant of the batch. Function B was next most significant. And so on, with F, "Human-ness," at the bottom of the list in importance, though still significant.

A close-up look at each of these cardinal functions will make clearer the targets which the leader should aim for. We will give some operational examples of methods which show how easily the targets can be hit by the person with enough flexibility to qualify as a leader.

A   Set group goals WITH the members
"Our boss asks our opinion frequently."
"He talks over changes with us."
"The boss uses some of our suggestions."
"He tips us off to things that are cooking."
"We have frequent group confabs on work problems."

B   Help them REACH the group goals
"My boss gives me help when I need it."
"He shows he is proud when we do a good job."
"He can help us on the technical details of a job."
"He listens to complaints, and takes care of them promptly."
"He sees that we have good equipment and materials on hand when we need them."

C COORDINATE the members
"Our boss delegates authority wisely."
"He lets us help each other."
"He gives us all a chance at choice jobs—no favorites."
"He lets us know how each of our jobs is important."
"He helps us work out things together."

D Help members FIT INTO THE GROUP
"Our boss understands the way we feel about things."
"He is good at seeing that the right people work to-
gether."
"He made me feel at home with the crew."
"Our leader takes a personal interest in us."
"He gives me a chance to do the work I am best at."

E INTEREST IN THE GROUP, not self
"Our leader is usually pulling for us."
"My boss does not stand between me and the com-
pany."
"He is good at getting us overtime, transfers, and
changes."
"He gives us sincere answers, and no run-around."
"Our leader will stick his neck out for us."

F "HUMAN-NESS"
"Our boss is easy to see and talk to."
"He is reasonable in what he asks, and in enforcing
rules."
"I feel free to talk over my personal problems with
him."
"He gives us a pat on the back when we do a good
job."
"I feel that I know him well."

Those six essential functions of successful personal leadership are worth pasting in one's hat. We are now going into each of them in detail, a chapter for each. The function found to count for most comes first, of course. Thus the next chapter is "Setting Goals WITH the Group."

4   *Setting goals ~~for~~ WITH the group*

What would you say is the leader's chief job? Get out the production? Keep everybody happy? Cut expenses? Keep the equipment in repair? Make a bigger profit? Find easier work procedures? Keep a jump ahead of competitors?

Many surveys of literally hundreds of ongoing groups agree on one leadership function which seems to outweigh all others. Reaching goals, such as those just mentioned, depends to a large extent upon the leader coming up to scratch in this function—setting goals WITH the group, rather than *for* the group.

"Carry out those boxes," is a close-range goal which the boss gives as an order. It is a goal he sets for the workers. We will see that such goals, when they are set for the workers, are not very impelling, no matter how logical or necessary the order may be. The goals that really impel are developed from within the work group itself.

We will see how a leader gets superior results when he sets goals WITH the workers who are necessary for reaching the goal. This sharing in making some of the plans gives the work group more purpose to work for. The workers come to feel more involved to make good and to reach the goal when they take part in deciding on that goal.

Records will be examined which indicate that sharing goal setting WITH the group lessens hostility and anxiety. Initiative and cooperation also appear to be improved. Followers and leader pull together more in the same direction when they decide together on common goals.

The reports summarized in this chapter will show ways in which the boss and his workers have developed goals together. These newer procedures are being used on a widening scale in all levels of leadership.

What happened with the Iowa housewives

Why don't more workers do the things that are plainly for their own interests in the long run? Such as following safety regulations, or using better job methods, or not stretching out work?

There is a general answer in some of the first experiments made in group forces. These pioneering experiments were aimed to find useful methods to lead Iowa housewives to improve the food value of their meals. That seemed like an easy assignment. Self-interest would "just naturally" make a housewife do what she should do to feed her family properly. Not like some workers who don't see why they should increase output so the company can make more money.

The obvious way to get the housewives to use more milk, for instance, was to let a nutrition expert tell them the facts. They'd believe him, and follow his impartial advice. Balanced diets would then sweep the state!

So they tried it. An expert from a famous hospital talked with groups of neighborhood housewives. Using words they all understood, he told why they should use more milk. It was a convincing talk: all science, no propaganda. Interesting, too. The women were astonished to learn how important milk was.

They started using more milk, did they? The lower bar on this chartoon shows how much of a goal the talk gave them.

More housewives followed their own decision than the expert's advice

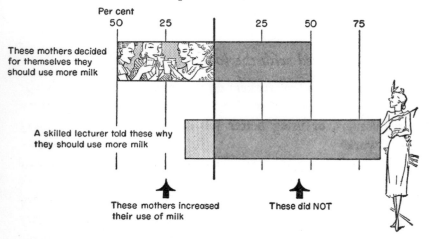

Only 16 per cent were doing anything about it. Not good enough. Perhaps another method might get more action.

Then a new method was worked out, and tried with similar groups of housewives. The same expert from the hospital was at these meetings. But this time he got the women to talk about the problem themselves. Town-meeting style.

They talked over among themselves "what housewives like us might do to use more milk." The expert answered their questions, but did not do much of the talking otherwise. They covered the same points that had been given in the lecture to the other women. And they met for the same length of time as the lecture groups.

These talkfest groups came to the inevitable conclusion that they should use more milk in their own families. But this goal was not one the expert had told them to aim for; the goal for these women was their own idea.

Did it make any difference who set the goal? Well, a month after these women set up a goal for themselves, half of them were actually using more milk. That was three times as large a share as when the specialist had tried to use his authority to set up the same goal for the other women.

The pattern to follow for better results

This little experiment is now a classic. Its findings have been confirmed by many similar tests. In general, the results are from two to ten times better when the people set the goal themselves.

This demonstration gives a pattern which can be followed for almost any objective the leader wants reached. The chief typist, for example, can get after her girls for making strike-overs, perhaps give a bonus for no strike-overs—or, she can get the girls together to talk over why strike-overs are a problem, and how to reduce the number of strike-overs. The chief will likely get better results by using the second way (unless the typists are so hostile toward her, or so upset by anxiety, that they can't help making strike-overs).

Any other occupation, or goals, can be substituted in this pattern. Just lead the group to decide upon a way for themselves, or upon the goal they want to reach.

People generally accept, and act upon, "our way" more

readily than they do "his way" or "what the boss wants." "Wanting to" has more motivating power than "having to."

When a goal is set WITH the group, the members are more likely to become self-directing with the leader, instead of against him. But lurking hostility or anxiety, of course, often complicates the situation.

The experiment on milk consumption was directed by Dr. Marian Radke-Yarrow, who is now with the National Institute of Mental Health (99).

How these pajama girls increased output after slumping

Let's imagine you are in charge of a group of girls working as pressers in a garment factory. You figure out a slight change which should help their work. A little change, such as putting the finished pieces in a shallow box instead of on the piece of cardboard they have been using. It is not like some of the big changes you know workers are inclined to resist.

We don't have to make believe about this. In one pajama factory the boss decided upon exactly that change, and told the pressers to do it the new way. The bottom curve in this chartoon shows how output dropped at once, and stayed down. What was wrong?

An answer is suggested in the way the girls began to argue with the methods engineer about the new method. They also started to sass their foreman, file grievances, and several quit their jobs. The girls' hostility had been turned loose by the autocratic style in which the minor change was made.

Having had no say-so in planning the change, the girls felt pushed around. They pushed back, developed anxiety, and found the work actually seemed much more difficult the new way. This was similar to the difficulty people have in understanding instructions when their hostility has been touched off.

Some of the higher-ups in this pajama factory knew about the experiments which had just been made with the Iowa

The girls took to the changed work method better when they helped plan it

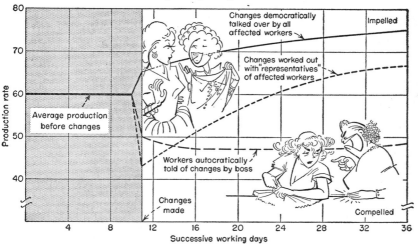

housewives. "Maybe our pressers would take to it better if we tried this in town-meeting style," they reasoned. So they got the girls together for a grass-roots session about another slight change which might be made in their work methods.

By this time there were only 13 of the original girls left. The others had quit because the job seemed too difficult when the box was substituted for the cardboard. This time the 13 pressers worked out the change themselves.

As soon as the remaining girls were asked to work out the

change, the human climate became different. This time the boss had shared the problem with them. It became the girls' problem, too, not just something for the wizards in the front office. The girls began to feel that they counted as individuals, and their feelings shifted favorably toward the work situation.

No longer the show of hostility; instead a mutual cooperation to make a go of the plan they had worked out—our plan, the girls felt, not the methods man's. No more sassing the boss, or complaining to the union.

Within three weeks, their production climbed higher than ever, as the top curve shows.

The growth of central planning and methods departments makes situations like this acute in many firms. These staff experts usually set the goals *for* rather than WITH the workers. This leaves the work group with no goals of its own—except for more wages and more benefits.

The goals the other fellow sets up for us are just chores. The goals we set for ourselves challenge us to settle down and dig. The worker who has no part in setting up some of his work goals is likely to aim at nothing in particular on the job, and hit it exactly.

This experiment in the pajama factory is another classic demonstration of group forces. It was reported originally by Drs. John R. P. French, Jr., and Lester Coch. It has been confirmed many times, by similar records from other groups, and for men workers as well as for women (23, 69).

Dr. H. G. Barnett's book, *Innovation: The Basis of Cultural Change*, published by the McGraw-Hill Book Company, Inc., is basic though difficult reading in this field.

Can we trick them into thinking it is their plan?

This is a good place to take a quick inventory to see what the leader is up against when setting some goals WITH a work group. We can start with this chartoon which tells a story about some offices in one of the world's largest corporations. This record is from Dr. Nancy C. Morse (94).

Slightly more than half of the office workers included in this study were allowed to make some decisions about their work methods and procedures. Most of these decisions allowed them were really minor, but still decisions.

Nearly half of these clerks were restricted in making any decisions. Not even minor ones. All decisions *for*, not WITH.

The clerks who were permitted to make some minor job decisions had the higher satisfaction with their jobs, as a rule.

Adding the two bottom blocks of this chartoon together, we find that three-fourths of the clerks wanted to make more decisions about their work. All in all, it seems to have been a restrictive rather than a permissive climate in this respect. Largely as a result of these findings, the company has experimented with changing the situation so that the clerks become more actively involved when changes or job decisions are made.

Here is the way things had been handled in this firm when changes were made in work methods (not shown in the chartoon):

A full explanation was made to 16 per cent of the clerks. Although the workers had no part in working out the changes, the boss did tell them the ins and outs after the higher-ups had decided on the changes.

No explanation was made to 26 per cent of the clerks. They were to catch on to the new method, and like it if they could.

Another 19 per cent were merely told how to do it the new way.

The remaining 39 per cent were given a partial explanation of the whys and wherefores of the changes.

Three-fourths of the office clerks wanted to make more decisions about their work

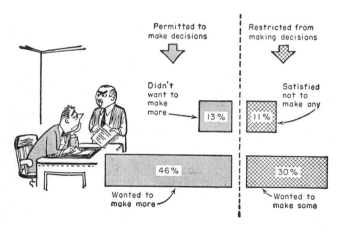

Dr. Morse found that the 16 per cent who were given full explanations about the changes were much more satisfied with the company as a place to work. They also were more likely to have high satisfaction with the details of their jobs.

Some leaders, who have a vague acquaintance with the way group forces operate, have tried stratagems to "sell" workers the changes or new goals. One stratagem sometimes tried is to include an obvious "bug" in the plan. The workers spot this flaw, the boss then throws out that part of the plan, and the workers are assumed to accept the rest of the plan as their own.

Another stratagem is to present a new plan by saying, "One of you suggested this some time ago."

For another stratagem, the boss lets the employees decide on some other goal, and assumes that will make them accept the unrelated plan he wants to put across.

But scattered records, and much practical experience, indicate that those stratagems seldom work. Quite often they backfire and make the climate worse. Apparently there is no substitute for sincerity and a democratic approach in setting goals WITH a work group, or other groups.

Not all of the planning can be done by the work groups, of course. But it almost always helps morale and production when the workers are in on some of the planning that affects their job details. Getting them in on the planning of, say, a departmental picnic cannot be expected to have much effect on raising their production goals. The goals set WITH the work groups need to be the direct goals, not evasive substitutes.

As the next chartoon demonstrates, the influence of the work group—"The Majority Effect"—is too powerful to bypass or to attempt to substitute "something just as good."

Why the checkerboard girls restricted their output

Quite often the boss feels that his workers lack initiative. But they may have plenty of initiative, though they are using it to reach goals which they got from themselves and not from their boss.

More output, for example, is probably the goal most bosses

try to instill in their work groups. Yet about half of factory workers use their initiative to keep output down to what they

The boss said "Speed up," other workers said "Slow down"—so they slowed down

consider "a reasonable level." Where do they get that conflicting goal that leads them to restrict output?

Dr. Stanley Schachter and associates looked for some answers to this question among girls who worked in teams of three, cutting and assembling checkerboards. The experiment was financed by the Carnegie Corporation, and done from the Laboratory for Research in Social Relations of the University of Minnesota (107).

When the girls started work on the new job, the boss told them that speed was important. He made it emphatic that lots of output was wanted. High production was the goal he set, or thought he had set for them.

Now one girl in each team was an "undercover agent." She had been secretly told to pass along prescribed slow-down messages to her teammates. This confederate was to give a slow-down message at the start and the middle of the last two work periods.

The middle column in this chartoon shows that output slumped 12 per cent as a result of the first two slow-down messages.

The column on the right shows that the next pair of slow-down messages dropped output 20 per cent below the base period.

Some of the actual slow-down messages used are on the chartoon. They seem like casual comments, or joking remarks. Yet such casual comments from fellow workers were followed, while the boss's high output goal was ignored.

. . . *and why they speeded up later*

There is another side to this checkerboard factory story. The undercover agents at another time passed along speed-up messages, such as: "Can't you hurry things a bit?" and "Can you step on it?" Otherwise the conditions were the same.

The work was speeded up by these casual speed-up messages. Output during the second period went up 50 per cent above the base period. And during the third period it was 96 per cent higher than in the base period. These were great gains, although the boss had assumed he had given the girls a goal of high output. But it was his goal, not theirs. They got their goals from interactions—casual remarks—with fellow workers.

This is one of many examples of the group's great power for setting goals, even when the group's pressure is slight. It has been said that the group's whisper carries more influence than the boss's shouts or threats.

Why didn't the slow-down messages produce as much change as the speed-up messages? Because these girls were not acquainted with each other before starting to work together, and the teams had not been together long enough to become cohesive—sticking together. The group conscience had not yet completely taken over the individuals' consciences. Had the group been in existence longer, and more cohesive, the slow-down effects might have been much greater (20, 103).

While most bosses hammer away for productivity, this goal has seldom been set WITH the work group. In consequence, the group conscience counts for more than the leader's orders. In some large offices, for example, high-producing employees were resented by 44 per cent of the clerks, admired by only 25 per cent. Among railroad laborers, a mere 16½ per cent had high pride in the productivity of their gangs (79, 94).

Government economists estimated some time ago that deliberate slowing down by workers costs consumers somewhere over a billion dollars a year (3).

How people come to "think" alike

It will be revealing to make a quick run-down of some other demonstrations of the strong forces groups exert in setting up goals which control individuals.

The power of the group kept the people from trusting their own eyes

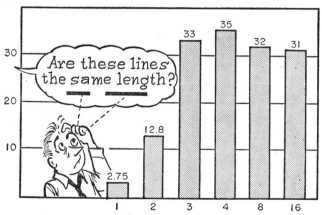

Per cent of times persons adopted the wrong estimate the group had made:

Could a group lead you to believe something was not as your own eyes saw it? You might be surprised! This chartoon illustrates a test on high-school graduates, all men, with good eyesight. They were to tell whether two lines were the same length or not. Most of the pairs of lines were noticeably different in length.

When these men were alone, they were almost 100 per cent correct in judging which line was longer.

But then they became the unsuspecting victims of group pressure. They sat in with a group, and all judged the lines. All the other people in the group were conspirators who had been told to call out wrong answers.

Each conspirator called out the wrong answer before the turn came for the innocent victim to report how the line lengths looked to him.

The first two columns on the left show that the victims were only slightly misled when one or two others preceded them with the wrong answer.

But when three or more others gave wrong answers before them, one-third of the victims gave in. They took the group's word, rather than what their eyes told them—the majority effect. It is significant that a group of three others was as powerful as a group of 16 for misleading the victims.

Some of the victims said later, after being told of the practical joke played on them, that the line lengths honestly seemed to change as they heard each of the others in the group call out the wrong answer. A few of the victims deliberately gave answers they felt were wrong; they did not want the group to think them queer. But most of the victims felt the group must be right, because it was unanimous.

This line-length experiment was performed by Dr. S. E. Asch, while a fellow of the Guggenheim Memorial Foundation (4).

Somewhat similar tests have been made when judging the size of a green rectangle. Dr. Everett W. Bovard, Jr., found in these tests that people tended to change their estimates to be

more like the one they were told a group of 20 to 30 people
had made (14).

. . . *and to distort facts*

When people realize they are "out of step" with what the
group believes, they often alter their recollections of facts, in
order to justify changing their original opinions to conform
to the majority. In experiments for the Office of Naval Research, Dr. Bertram H. Raven found there was considerable
distortion of facts, even when the person's opinion was his
own secret—distorting in an effort to convince themselves, or
to soothe their consciences. When their opinion was to be
made public to the group of 10 to 14 others, the tendency to
stretch facts was doubled (100)!

Other experiments, by Dr. Carl I. Hovland and associates,
supported by the Rockefeller Foundation, have shown that
people who are wrapped up in a particular group are not very
likely to change their beliefs, or goals, that are held by the
groups to which they feel they belong, or to which they feel
attracted. And other of these experiments show that trying to
argue people into changing goals which were anchored to
their groups backfired; the persons became all the more con-
vinced that the group was right (49, 63).

Groups inevitably develop some goals of their own—how
quickly was illustrated by the checkerboard girls. The successful leader learns to develop some goals WITH the group.
He does not assume that they have all the goals he thinks they
should have. Or that they will accept the goal merely because
he gives them logic-tight reasons why they should.

The best substitute for a "group think"

The housewives using more milk, and the girls pressing pajamas, illustrate the most effective way yet found to lead a group. That was by setting up some goals WITH them. Some goals about which they felt personally concerned. And which hit directly on the problem, not something offside, such as planning a picnic.

The project concerned the group's daily work or daily life, not running the business in general. Close-to-home projects.

The next best way to having a "group think" on the project is for the leader to be able to read the mind of the group. Seriously. Much as a skilled secretary can read her executive's mind and know what he would dictate in reply to much of his mail. Not as the man who is said to have given his wife a monkey wrench for a birthday present.

Dr. Theodore M. Newcomb and colleagues have found that successful leaders have a fairly accurate idea of how their followers feel about things as a group. These leaders sense how their followers think, without hearing them express themselves in a "group think." As a result, these leaders can make decisions which are acceptable to their followers (22).

This chartoon pictures the accepted leaders' superiority in knowing how their groups felt about topics of concern to the purposes of the groups. Some of the groups were concerned primarily with politics and economics, some with medical questions. This chartoon is for religious groups.

The chosen leaders greatly excelled in their ability to "take the pulse" of the members on topics the group considered important, without having to ask the members how they felt about things. The leaders were more in tune with the goals

Those voted leaders excelled in reading the members' minds

Superiority of
leaders in judging
group opinion:

Compared with
Nonleaders

Compared with
those ignored
by group

toward which the members wanted to make headway. But the leaders were not much superior in knowing how the members felt on topics which were offside for the group as a whole—such as the size of family they wanted, or the make of automobile they preferred.

The leader who is sensitive to group objectives is less likely to lose his influence if he sometimes arbitrarily sets up project goals for them. He will be able to set up a goal they can wholeheartedly accept and get behind. He can put himself in the other fellow's shoes.

Getting the right picture of what their workers want

There is strong evidence from many sides that the successful leader is usually aware of the aspirations, feelings, and ideals of his followers. He senses what their unspoken goals are, and understands their problems as the followers see them. He leads to a large extent by taking his cues from the group he is leading. He senses that his wife would prefer a kitchen knife to a monkey wrench on her birthday.

Empathy is the word used for this knack of tuning in on the other person. The leader who has his ear to the ground and knows what goals his followers are seeking, is said to have high empathy. But the boss who makes poor guesses about what the workers have on their minds, has low empathy. The one with low empathy has good chances of missing the target when he sets up goals for the group. It is not surprising that low sensitivity to workers' attitudes goes hand in hand with low productivity (10, 95, 122).

This raises the question of how good first-line leaders are in sensing what workers want from their work and from their bosses. Workers almost never express their goal motivations in so many words. The boss has more or less to guess, or read minds, to know the aspirations that move his workers.

Numerous reports have shown that bosses make many wild guesses about their workers' goals. For a single illustration we will outline what was found in the case of blue-collar workers in one company. The investigators first determined the more important things the workers themselves wanted from their jobs. Then the fifty-five foremen of these same workers told how they figured the workers valued the same things as goals (60).

The following percentages show how the bosses over-guessed, or underguessed, the valuation their workers placed on each of the factors listed:

	Per cent
Overguessed:	
Easy work	200
High pay	74
Comfortable work conditions ..	27
Good boss	4
Steady work	3
Underguessed:	
Opportunity to advance	25
Opportunity to learn	39

Notice that the underguessed factors bear on the social aspects of the jobs. They are tied in with the social force of prestige, and are a common cause of anxieties that are not directly expressed. Workers value these opportunities highly, because of the chance given to move upward in their work groups and become persons of a little more distinction. The advertising expert understands the power of these forces more than most production executives do.

In most factories where comparisons have been made, it has been found that the union stewards have a more accurate picture (better empathy, better guesses) of what impels the workers than the foremen do.

The foremen, in turn, usually have better empathy than do the higher-ups. This may be because the first-level bosses have been through the mill, and are guided somewhat by recollections of their own feelings before their rise to a boss's status. This may be an influence in workers' feeling that more foremen than higher-ups are fair and square (103).

People with the authoritarian make-up have also been found to have the wrong picture of most people's goals. Authoritarians have a good enough picture of other authoritarians, but are much out of focus when picturing the democratically inclined portion of the population (37, 56).

Beliefs to straighten out

Engineering graduates, who had only a few years' experience in business, have been found to have a high percentage of wrong guesses about the things that motivate workers. Patrick C. Farbro has reported the following misconceptions held by 244 beginning leaders in a modern electronics plant. The percentages indicate how blurred their picture was. In reading this list, bear in mind that each statement is incorrect in the light of what is known today about human relations (66, Chapter 20).

Incorrect belief they held	Per cent who held it
It is undesirable to put plates on each important piece of equipment to show its value and cost of operation ...	55
It is undesirable to ask employees to recommend acquaintances for jobs with the company	48
It is desirable to fine workers when they break rules ...	37
How fellow workers treat a man will have nothing to do with how he likes his job	33

Incorrect belief they held	Per cent who held it
It does not reflect on the boss in case a worker goes over the boss's head	33
An honest worker will not go on strike if the company pays good wages	31
It is a good thing to "make an example" of one worker in order to prevent trouble with others	28
The best way to be sure rules are obeyed is to put some teeth in them	27
If a man is capable of doing a good job, he will be interested in it whether the boss stimulates him or not ..	25
It is undesirable to ask workers how they feel about the way the company treats them	23
The average worker doesn't care whether the thing he makes is useful or not	22
The kind of work a person does has little effect on his social standing	21
Sympathizing with a worker's difficulties does no good but to encourage him to complain	21
Inefficient workers should be told to get busy, or get out	20

Could we get those young engineers to have a more accurate picture by bluntly telling them which of their ideas were wrong? "Telling them," even when done by an expert, has not been found to produce much change—as with the Iowa housewives. But there are ways to use "group thinks" which do seem to help leaders improve their empathy. In the following chapter we will look into the use of climate and group thinks in setting goals.

5 *The use of "group thinks" and climate in setting work goals*

This is a continuation of the preceding chapter on setting goals WITH the group. The newer ways for setting work goals can be lumped into two general methods. While we can separate the methods for study, in actual practice they are intertwined and go together for best results.

The one approach, or method, is to create a human climate that is favorable for cooperation and understanding mutually shared objectives. The other general method is to use project sessions in which leader and followers have a "group think" together to solve some problem they share in common. The success of a group think appears to depend to a large extent upon the climate, as we learned in connection with the bargaining sessions.

Climate and group thinks are more roundabout ways, and take more time and patience than the direct "tell them what to do and how to do it" method. But they have proved to be much more effective in getting results, as well as in strengthening human relations.

There are a few conditions, however, under which the direct approach has at times shown up as better than these roundabout approaches:

1. When an emergency required immediate action.
2. When the group was of low skill and ability.
3. When the followers were fanatically devoted to some religious figure or political savior.

The over-all human climate that helps

The climate that is favorable for setting goals with the group is democratic, not dictatorial; permissive, not restrictive; group-centered, rather than leader-centered; equalitarian, not authoritarian. The leader creates a sincere atmosphere which stimulates followers to open up and swap ideas and share some secrets with him. Hostility is at a minimum; unfortunately it is seldom absent from leader-follower relationships in business and industry.

The leader has been found to have most influence in upgrading group goals when he establishes a permissive climate, when he asks for their suggestions (and uses some of them); less when he tries to sell his followers into accepting only his suggestions. Throwing the book of rules at them, and handing out discipline, chokes off a group think before it starts.

There is not much exaggeration in saying that the climate counts for more than the desirability of the goal for everyone concerned. Groups cut off their own noses and sabotage a goal that is in their self-interest, when the climate arouses more than a minimum of hostility. People are motivated by their interactions in a total situation, not by the goal someone sets for them. The human climate permeates the total situation, and we will come back to that aspect shortly, and spell it out in detail.

Close-at-hand problems

For a group think, the leader tosses in some problem or project bearing on the group's work, and they all chew it over. The project does not deal with a problem in another department, or with higher-up problems such as finances or general policies. These freewheeling sessions try to solve some problem shared at the local level, by both followers and leader. Here are some examples from recent business experience:

"Traffic conditions are getting worse as we drive to work mornings. What can we do to ease this up?" the supervisor asked. One crew member suggested using a helicopter, and that got a laugh. The session reached a decision that it would be desirable to stagger opening hours, thus avoiding the traffic to other factories and offices. It worked out to their satisfaction, and with management's O.K. spread to other departments. Can you recall the squawks there used to be when the same change was ordered directly by the sensible general manager?

"The Federal inspectors are rejecting so much of our output that we will go into the red, and we may lose this contract. There must be something we can do about it. What ideas do you folks have?" Several sessions were used to thresh this out, and there was much talking about it between sessions. The workers finally reached the decision that some quality-control system was needed, and that two of the production machines should be rebuilt, or junked. They turned down one suggestion for bribing the inspectors, and another to toss the inspectors into the canal behind the plant. Quite different from what usually happens when the boss puts on a one-man drive for quality control.

"We are going to have to change the shop from repairing steam locomotives to doing nothing but diesel work. This old shop just isn't laid out for diesel jobs." That statement of the problem started the mechanics on a series of lunch-hour and after-work sessions. On their own, they worked out a new layout, and made a mock-up model for changing over the shop. They reached a better solution, the directors thought, than did the architects who had been retained to draw plans for the same change-over.

Solve mutual problems rather than dispute beliefs

Some leaders imagine these group thinks are a close relative to a political argument, and that the sessions should be used for converting the workers' political and economic thinking. That is precisely what a group think should not be.

The purpose is not so much to change their beliefs, as to solve some practical problem facing both group and leaders. When people suspect that the leader is bent on changing their opinions, there is less change of opinion than otherwise. Similarities rather than differences need the emphasis.

Dr. Thomas N. Ewing has reported experiments in which some of the groups were given the impression that the leader was out to change their opinions. He found practically no change in opinion when the people thought the person talking was out to prove them wrong. But the groups who were led to think the identical facts agreed with their ideas were influenced five times as much (30).

Occasionally the leader has an inclination to talk mostly to the one or two members he feels are most in need of being converted. It has been found that the tendency of most people in a group think is to do just that—to direct their remarks to specific individuals. But Dr. Robert F. Bales has found that the person who emerges as the leader in a group think is the one who addresses the largest share of his comments to the group as a whole. Apparently the leader is more aware of the existence of the group as a group, and is not inclined to feud with individuals. He may help the group to think more alike, also, because he talks *to* the group rather than *at* an individual (7).

The leader who is overly zealous to have the group come up with the "right" decision is also likely to give only one side of the case. Dr. Carl I. Hovland directed a series of experiments which showed that the group changes more in the direction wanted, however, when the leader gives both sides of the question. Giving only one side was found to be effective only with the members who had felt that way originally (49).

The urge to dispute is something else the leader of a group think has to control in himself. This has been demonstrated in tests with groups of Air Force officers by Dr. Thomas F. Staton. There were a dozen men in each group think (112).

As the chartoon shows, only 6 per cent of the remarks made by the men who emerged as leaders were of a disputing nature. But the officers considered nonleaders made almost twice that amount of argumentative remarks.

Some of the nonleaders were also inclined to push their pet ideas. Some of their disputing was an effort to get the thinking of the group back to their own favorite ideas. One-track minds, so to speak.

A group is eager to make progress toward its goal in a group think. Disputing, or harping on one idea, prevents this headway.

The men who disputed less were looked upon as leaders

Disputing
points made
by others:

10.4%

6.2%

Rated as leaders
by the others

Not rated
as leaders
by others

An easy start in a free-and-easy climate

Most work groups also have no experience with these shirt-sleeve conferences. Many are flabbergasted the first time the boss makes one of "his" problems also their problem. The followers may seem tongue-tied, or without suggestions to solve the problem, at the start. But there are almost always resources worth tapping in the work group. In that locomotive repair shop, for one case, the mechanics had much more know-what than the consulting architects had.

Experience indicates that it is wise to use easy steps when starting project sessions. It takes some time for the workers to get used to the democratic sharing of some problems. Easy projects, or problems, are usually recommended as starters: "That water cooler gets in everybody's way; there must be a better location for it."

Easy projects will not overtax the abilities of the group, and the participants will have a feeling of getting somewhere. No point in handing them a knotty mess which will be beyond their depth; that would only add to any anxiety.

The problems usually deal with some detail about which they are concerned in their daily work. Not the long-range problems which keep management scratching its head. The group-think projects take up methods rather than policies.

The think sessions are sometimes around a table, like the board of aldermen. At other times they are seemingly spur-of-the-moment affairs, while workers and boss are huddled over a work bench, or grouped in a corridor.

Most first-level confabs are not around a table. They take place right at the side of a machine, or in a corner of the shop, or while shooting the breeze at coffee break or lunch. There is usually a casual atmosphere, with no gavel-banging to call the meeting to order. The free-and-easy atmosphere is presumed to stimulate the flow of ideas and interactions, and to minimize social distance and hostility.

The leader's task at the start

It will help crystallize the methods if we look in on 22 group thinks. Not all sessions are alike, but on the average they tend to follow a pattern. The pattern charted here was reported by Drs. Robert F. Bales and Fred Stroudtbeck, and is based on findings from the Harvard Laboratory of Social Relations (8).

None of the participants had had much previous experience in group thinks. A wide assortment of problems was taken up by the various groups. The average interactions probably followed much the same pattern as for other groups with only normal hostilities who get together for think sessions for the first time. As participants have more experience in these, and develop cohesiveness, the sessions go more smoothly, and the quality of their thinking improves greatly (78).

These 22 group thinks were slow in getting up steam. So the three phases pictured in this chartoon were not of equal length. After the records were in, the sessions were divided into phases so there was the same number of interactions, not minutes, in each phase. The first phase took the longest time, the last phase the shortest. They started out in low gear, but were really moving toward the end. There is much practical significance in the way the nature of their interactions changed from one phase to the next.

During the first phase there were large chunks of silence. The people sat, bewildered and thinking. This silence was probably not due to hostility, though in some cases it is a version of a sit-down strike. In the conferences pictured, however, there were about 50 per cent more positive than negative interactions during the first phase (not charted).

Getting their bearings, and collecting their thoughts, prob-

How the discussion shifted during the conferences

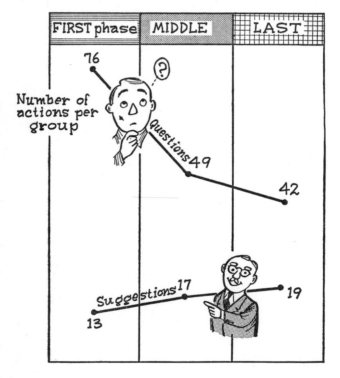

ably caused the slow start. They asked questions galore—six times as many questions asked in this phase as suggestions offered.

During these early phases, the leader seemed to function best when he acted as a consultant, or resource person. He answered questions when he was able to, but did not himself suggest a solution. Perhaps he knew what the solution should be, but was careful not to give the impression that he was pressuring them to agree with him by telling them the solution he had in mind. The aim of the sessions was to work out a project, shoulder-to-shoulder, not for the leader to talk them into accepting a solution they hadn't yet thought of for themselves.

The leader took advantage of the periods of silence to observe facial expressions, for reasons we will see shortly. Had he broken the silence to put in his oar, it would have distracted their thinking and might have given the impression he was a steam roller, after all. The thing for the group to beat was the problem, not the leader.

How the leader stimulates thinking

Let's follow through the second and third phases to see what happened. Questions eased off rapidly. The folks were getting a better understanding of the problem.

And during these later phases there was a steady rise in the suggestions—bright ideas—for ways to lick the problem.

The effective leader stimulates this flow of bright ideas by repeating each one when it is offered. He often rephrases it, to make its meaning clearer. He often lists it on a blackboard, or on a sheet of paper, so that none of the members who advance suggestions feel overlooked.

For this rephrasing, and for giving really clarifying answers to questions, the leader needs a good vocabulary. This was demonstrated by Major Norman E. Green with groups of military officers who spent an entire day discussing problems of leadership and group efficiency. There were 9 to 10 men in each think group (36).

This chartoon shows how much better the most influential

A good vocabulary made them more influential in the project sessions

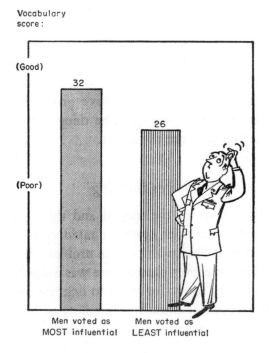

Vocabulary score :

(Good)

32

26

(Poor)

Men voted as   Men voted as
MOST influential   LEAST influential

men in these sessions were in understanding and using words. Some of the least influential may have had good ideas to offer, but low verbal skill cut down their effectiveness in influencing the group.

Some groups are composed of a few people with big vo-cabularies, and others with small vocabularies. The group thinking in such a case will tend to be lopsided. In such cases, the leader repeats what the big-word member says, but in little words which everyone can understand. He may also need to help the person of few words to explain his ideas. That helps the group make headway.

How the leader increases positive interactions

The leader does not give a touchy follower a chance to infer that the boss rejected the suggestion as soon as it was made. Some of the earlier suggestions may be stupid, but let the group decide later which ones to put in the wastebasket.

The group thinks produce best when the leader sets a climate that keeps questions and suggestions flowing. The time to evaluate the ideas comes later. It is quick death to a group think for the leader to pick and choose from ideas as they are uttered.

In the 22 sessions charted earlier, there was a great rise in positive interactions as the confabs went on. Examples: Giving help to others, complimenting others, agreeing with them, laughing and joking. Signs of a favorable climate—participants not only more at ease, but also feeling they are making headway.

The thinking during the first phase is looked upon as being mostly individual thinking. Sometime later, if the session has been properly handled, there is a transition to a more truly group thinking. Examples: "There are points we could use from both John's and Alfred's ideas." "Wish Elsie would tell us more about her plan." "Frank suggested a gravity feed, Mac a feed from the left side—why can't we combine both ways?"

When this stage of group thinking is reached, the interactions speed up. One member's suggestion unloosens a related idea from another. It may become exciting as they get to thinking on the same track.

As this kind of group thinking comes to the fore, there is a gain in we-feeling for the time being. Cooperativeness rather than each man defending his own pet notions. Getting shoulder to shoulder, rather than most of them against a few others.

When this stage of group thinking is reached there is also an improvement in the quality of the suggestions made. Fuller use is being made of the resources—the know-how—of the members. In view of this gain in the quality of the ideas coming out in later phases, the actual gain is probably much greater than the bare numbers shown on the chartoon of the 22 sessions.

How large a group? How long a conference?

Several other factors which affect the quality of the decisions from a group think have been measured.

Size of the group is one factor. Small groups are easier to get together, and some leaders say they are easier to handle. And sometimes it is claimed that a large group "talks too much to get anywhere."

Dr. Irving Lorge studied this with several hundred Air Force officers, all majors or lieutenant colonels. Some of them worked in group thinks of 6 to 8 men, others in larger groups of 12 to 13 men. The quality of decisions reached by the larger groups was decidedly superior. The large groups also made

62 per cent more general recommendations, and had four times as many specific details for action in their reports.

By and large, doubling the size of these staff groups doubled the quality of their decisions. Adding more members naturally brought in more ideas and different points of view to make the group think productive.

In a variation of this experiment, Dr. Lorge also found that a session that lasted 100 minutes produced decisions (goals) about twice the quality of a 50-minute session (78).

Help from the minority or timid member

Another factor which affects the quality of decisions reached in a group think is for the leader to take pains to see that the timid, bashful, even unpopular member takes part in the discussions. The leader should look upon those present not just as people, but also as participants—and should get them to take part; not merely to keep all happier, but actually to improve the quality of the decision.

This was shown by an ingenious demonstration conducted by Dr. Norman R. F. Maier (82).

How accurately do you think a group could solve this problem: "John bought a horse for $60 and sold it for $70. Then he bought it back for $80, but sold it the next day for $90. How much did he make, or lose?"

Dr. Maier had half of the groups discuss this problem without a leader. The other groups had leaders who had been instructed to get all members to take part. As the chartoon shows, the groups which had the leaders ended up with significantly more correct answers. Why?

In the leaderless confabs, the bashful or meek member who might know how to get the answer, often did not have a chance. The talk was a leaderless free-for-all. Although there

Better group decisions when a leader gave the minority a chance

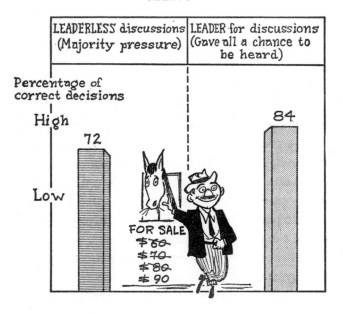

LEADERLESS discussions (Majority pressure)	LEADER for discussions (Gave all a chance to be heard)

Percentage of correct decisions

High

72

84

Low

FOR SALE
$~~60~~
$~~70~~
$~~80~~
$ 90

were 5 or 6 people in each leaderless group, not all of them could be participants—the aggressive members of the group dominated the sessions.

But the appointed leaders had been asked to use democratic methods and get all to participate. Under this condition the Little Fellows and the Bashful Boys got a chance to help the group find the correct answer. Fuller use was made of the resources within the group. Getting the minority to take active part may upgrade the quality of the final consensus.

(The correct answer, in case you are wondering, is $20 profit.)

Getting hostility out of the atmosphere

But don't get the impression that a group think is all milk and honey after it gets started. In the 22 conferences charted earlier, for instance, there was a slight rise in negative interactions as a session neared its close. Examples: Disagreeing with others, arguing, not talking, and signs of tenseness.

The rise in these negative interactions is looked upon as owing to some people's having to give up pet ideas, or becoming envious of someone who came up with a better idea.

But some of the negative interactions are merely the ventilation of rivalries and hostilities that are ordinarily kept under cover.

Although there is a slight rise in negative interactions toward the close of the typical session, the rise of positive interactions is much greater. The net effect in the final phase is that positive interactions smother out the negative, nearly four to one.

The rise in negative interactions, however, points up the leader's need to be on watch so he can pour oil on the waters if they become troubled. An effective move at such a juncture is to recall to the group one of the facetious suggestions that was made earlier, such as solving the traffic jam with helicopters, or tossing the inspectors into the canal. Such silly suggestions can ultimately have serious use.

Some experienced leaders of group thinks like to have an assistant detailed to toss in a wisecrack if the session becomes tense. And one purpose of the leader's observing facial expressions and the tone of voices is to gauge moods as well as how the various suggestions seem to register with the participants.

Winding up the conference

How about taking a vote to see how the group stands at the close of the session? That depends upon many conditions, and is usually not necessary with work groups.

As the group goals are upgraded through the swapping of ideas, the behavior of most of the participants will be modified without a formal vote. The suggestions on which the closing phase concentrates will tip off all but the thickest skinned about how the group thinks about it.

This consensus has a powerful influence, even upon those who actually don't like the way the group concluded. Recall the power of the majority effect in the preceding chapter.

How about the leader drawing conclusions for them at the close? That is usually not needed in work groups, and may backfire, depending upon the human climate in the establishment. The voice of the leader may not count as much as the followers' sensing how the group as a whole feels—recall the checkerboard girls.

A summing up, however, may help clear up some fuzzy points, especially if the leader is able to talk their language in rephrasing. And if he is careful to mention that the points originated with Alfred, Elsie, or Mac, or with some person the members look upon as an unofficial leader or pacemaker.

Or, depending upon the situation, by asking one of the popular participants to sum up for them. These procedures help emphasize that the goal was set by the group, not railroaded through by the boss.

Getting on to the know-how

Ordinarily it takes a good many tries before both leader and followers have the knack of working together in a group think. It is usually easier for the group to get into the swing. It may take several fruitless sessions, however, to thaw out a dispirited (anxious) or hostile group—situations where the emphasis should be on changing the climate.

Conferences with skilled and higher-level groups seem to make most headway. This may be because they have more abilities to draw upon for making constructive suggestions. The higher-level groups may also be accustomed to a more democratic work climate.

The autocratic leader usually has the most trouble making a go of goal-setting group thinks. It is his style to give the answers, rather than draw others out and listen to them. He may be impatient for instant results, and may want to alter their entire economic philosophy in two short sessions. It is usually difficult for the autocratic person to be a feeler, and to take his cues from the group—to analyze their facial expressions without wanting to give them a talking to, for instance.

A few high-level executives, aware of their limitations in handling group thinks, and aware also of the value of such get-togethers, have chosen assistants who are especially adept in upgrading group goals. An increasing share of these assistants have had special training in conducting group thinks. A few of the larger universities now give such training. This is usually in workshops which give practical experience. The National Training Laboratory for Group Development has been operating at Bethel, Maine, during the summers since 1947 (118).

Many supervisory training courses are also using these methods to sharpen the skills of first-line leaders in handling informal thinks right on the job. We summarized some of these in the second chapter.

How to test the climate

Back, now, to that question of the human climate which is a potent factor in determining whether leader and followers share goals.

A stranger visiting a factory or office for the first time can usually sense this climate. It is not a matter of housekeeping, or air conditioning, or odors, or decorations. In one plant there will be furtive glances at the boss, tenseness, and other signs of strained relations. In another the workers and foremen seem to be much more at home with each other.

To get a line on the style of climate, use is made of workers' accounts of the operational relationships between employees and their bosses. The following are statements which describe climates favorable for the joint setting of work goals, in contrast with what might be termed one-man rule. Group thinks work well in the climate conveyed by these verbatim statements.

"Our boss asks our opinion frequently."
"He often gives us a chance to be on our own."
"He lets us know about things that may be coming up."
"I feel free to make work suggestions."
"The boss uses some of our work suggestions."

"Our leader gives recognition for good work."
"He talks over changes with us."
"I feel free to talk over personal problems with him."
"He is easy to see about job problems."
"Our boss has frequent meetings with the work group."

"He is reasonable in what he expects from us."
"Our boss listens to us."
"He is reasonable in enforcing the rules."
"We can count on him in the tough spots."
"He shows he is proud when we do a good job."

"Our boss lets us help each other out."
"He lets us work out things together."
"He understands the way we feel about things."
"Our boss is usually pulling for the crew."
"He listens to our gripes, and takes care of them."

*   *   *

After this bonus chapter on setting goals WITH the group, we turn next to the leadership objective that is slightly second in importance to this. That is "Helping the team reach their goals."

6   *Helping the team reach their goals*

Does only about one out of three work groups have pride in its productivity? Why not more? Maybe they do not have goals for high output. And, maybe they are marking time until the leader gives them the help they want in order to make some progress; it is this angle we will consider in this chapter.

The research summaries we will scan show that followers expect the leader to help them reach goals. The goals may be shared by the entire group, or they may be the individual's own goal. Whichever it is, when the leader does what the followers think he should for them to make headway toward the goals, then both production and morale are on the way up.

We will find that followers do *not* expect the leader to help by working beside them at the same tasks they are doing.

They want their leader to play a different role than that of just another workman. They want him to do things for the team that the workers are not capable of doing, or are not in a position to do for themselves.

Although the team wants a word in deciding some things that come close to home in their work, they want their leader to have superior power in solving their problems, and in smoothing out the path so they can make headway. It is not exactly paternalism, but akin to it. We will put the micro-scope on some of these "higher activities" of leaders that enable the team to make the progress it wants to make.

As has been pointed out, the football coach does not put on shoulder pads and buck the line himself. His job is to do something "higher" than play in the game himself.

Better output when the boss spent more time supervising

One goal all work groups have is to turn out some produc-tion. Sometimes the production goal the workers accept is as high as the boss wants it to be. But, in about half the cases, the crew has a secret goal that is below what the boss wants. This causes some anxiety for both boss and worker (24).

Are workers likely to reach a higher output if the boss rolls up his sleeves and helps out at the bench beside them? The chartoon shows what happened in groups of semiskilled office clerks and railroad laborers, as reported by Dr. Nathan Mac-coby. Altogether there were 600 workers, and 84 first-line bosses (79).

Half of these bosses spent more time supervising than help-ing out in actual production. The other half spent most of their time working directly on the job, the same as the workers.

The cuts of pie in this chartoon show how the bosses who had high-output crews were mostly those who did not do much of the production work themselves. But with the low-output crews it was the opposite—most of their bosses pitched in to help get out the work.

This is difficult to believe at first glance. The crews were small, only about eight persons. When the boss worked side by side with them, the crew strength was considerably increased. Yet output was cut. How come?

The bosses of high-production units spent more time in supervising than doing the work themselves

HIGH-output offices.   LOW-output offices

Bosses who spent
more than half of
time SUPERVISING

72.5%   32.5%

27.5%   67.5%

Who spent more
than half of time
HELPING DO
THE WORK

One obvious reason was the workers' feeling that the boss lacked confidence in them, so was working beside them. Or, they felt, he was dissatisfied with the way they were doing the job, and their anxiety was aroused. Some workers got the idea he was trying to set a faster pace for them, and hostility was felt. Workers commonly resent a boss sticking his nose into their work. All these interactions cut down the will to work, and made some workers jittery or bunglesome.

Better work when they feel the boss is helping them reach work goals

Another reason is less obvious. But it is more important in connection with helping the team reach their goals. This is tied in with the social forces which are operating in teams. Some of these forces lead members to feel they will reach their goals better if they have a leader, not merely another part-time worker. It is a truism that groups want a leader, although they may not want the particular one they happen to have.

Team members expect this leader they want to perform different operations from those of the rank-and-file. They expect the boss to play a different role, not to do routine production. They expect him to facilitate their efforts and give them support toward reaching their goals (11).

The work group expects their leader to:

Have materials on hand when needed	An expediter
Get them good tools and surroundings ...	A retriever
Coordinate the members of the crew	A smoother-outer
Help them solve personal problems	A counselor
Help them solve job problems	A consultant, or expert
Keep them informed about what's cooking	A communicator
Watch out for their interests	A protector
Develop their skills	A trainer

They also expect the leader, if he is successful, to work harder and longer than the followers. But at the leader's functions, not at the routine operations on their own jobs (44).

Thus workers expect the boss to be a specialist who helps them reach goals. These specialties are in two broad classes: (a) mobilizing the human resources within the group, and (b) mobilizing the equipment and materials needed to reach the goals.

The leaders' results, not their intentions, were what helped

One of the "higher" things followers expect their leaders to do is look after the interests of the individuals, as well as of the team as a whole: a caretaker, or paternal function of leadership—the "papa will take care of you" idea.

In terms of a work team, this includes going to bat for them. But the records indicate that just going to bat is not enough. This finding came out in an analysis, by Dr. Donald C. Pelz, of the morale of 8,000 workers in a large electric firm (97).

The morale of these workers was checked against many of the actions and methods of their immediate bosses. Perhaps the bosses who made most use of good human-relations methods would have crews with the best morale.

The records didn't come out that way. Some of the foremen who used good human-relations procedures did have high-morale gangs. But other bosses who used about the same methods had low-morale crews.

So the investigators looked into another angle. Some of the bosses had influence with their higher-ups. When these high-influence foremen went to bat, they usually got what they wanted for their workers. Naturally the workers under such a powerful foreman felt he could help them reach goals, and this power made them more satisfied.

There were other bosses who seldom got an O.K. from the

The foremen who could make good on their promises had better worker morale

Cases where
actions of
supervisor
raised morale.

68%

·29%

Supervisors with
LOW power

Supervisors with
HIGH power

higher-ups. These low-influence bosses couldn't make good on their promises to the men. And sometimes they foolishly promised too much. But generally, they simply lacked the weight to get management to approve their requests—double-crossed by the controller, is the way some workers expressed it.

Remember that there was no real difference in the human-relations methods of these foremen. What counted was that those pictured on the right had (or could get) the authority to do the extras that helped their teams feel the boss could get them somewhere.

It was about the same with white-collar workers as with blue-collar. Throughout the firm, morale was highest where the boss could make good on his promises and not have the rug pulled out from under him by his chief.

Followers want their leaders to have power

Other reports show that workers do not feel they have much power themselves to get the things they need from management to make progress toward their goals. Dr. John James has found that workers on strike, however, feel they have more of this power than do similar union workers who are not on strike (53).

And experiments supported by the Research Institute of the University of Oklahoma have shown that followers have great expectations from the people they look upon as their leaders. The followers greatly overestimated how well their leaders could do a simple act of muscular skill. And they also underestimated the same skill of people they shunned as leaders. By feeling their leader has a few superman qualities, the team shows less anxiety about making headway (43, 110).

As companies have grown larger, there has been a tendency to "tighten the organization." A favorite way to do this is to take some authority from the first-line bosses and give it to a staff expert. Nowadays the first-line boss may not have authority to adjust complaints. Similar limitations on his power have, in many instances, whittled down his size in the workers' eyes to the extent that they doubt if he can really help them make headway.

Getting goal-motivated spurts in the marmalade factory

It is easy to understand how a feeling of making headway will boost morale. It is an encouraging feeling that lessens anxiety.

This same feeling of progress has also been shown to help production. Individuals, as well as teams, make more effort when they see they are achieving something in the direction in which they are headed.

This principle has been extensively applied by consultants of the National Institute of Industrial Psychology, London, in the spectacular output gains they have brought about in British factories and offices.

An example was the group of girls preparing fruit in a marmalade factory. Under the original scheme, a full day's work was piled in front of each girl at the start of the day. That mountain of fruit made the job seem like an endless activity that got nowhere slowly (127).

Then one simple change was made by the psychologists. The girls were given a small trayful of fruit at a time to work on. This almost doubled their output!

A stop-watch study might have indicated that the new method would waste time, as one tray was changed for another. There would also be avoidable steps in removing and bringing trays. But the results in output, which have been demonstrated many times, bring home the point that people, unlike machines, are goal-motivated—or can be goal-motivated if the work is arranged for that purpose.

Each small trayful presented a goal. During the work spell, each tray gave a close-range goal, or "achievement point." When a tray was completed, a sub-goal had been reached, and there was a stimulating feeling of getting ahead with the job. What had been a daily grind became more a pursuit of achievement points.

Goal-motivated behavior is featured by spurts, when extra steam is turned on (66, Chapters 2, 8).

1. There is an *initial spurt* each time a fresh batch is tackled.
2. A *make-up-for-lost-time spurt* after an interruption, or when one becomes aware of a slump.
3. And a *finish-line* spurt when the goal comes in sight.

When the work was reorganized for the marmalade girls, the number of these spurts during a day was multiplied. The momentum this gave them was shown by the gain in output, despite the time lost in changing trays.

Quotas as a way of making headway

Work quotas are another example of goals. Sometimes these goals are set in an arbitrary fashion, without the team participating. And the quota may be set unreasonably high, on the assumption that it will serve as an incentive to work harder. But when workers feel that the bosses are making unreasonable demands, it has been found that the team lowers its output. More blue-collar than white-collar bosses are seen as unreasonable by their workers (60).

Assembly-line operations are a problem. It is usually difficult to supply sub-goals, or achievement points, to encourage the workers to sense they are making headway (126).

The stimulating effects of close-at-hand achievement points, and of reasonable quotas, is an illustration of some of the "higher" things the leader can do to lead a team to feel it is making progress. And followers support the person they feel is helping them get somewhere.

Providing a variety of tasks

Another of the "higher" things the leader does to help workers sense they are making headway is to provide variety in the job. The girl in a one-girl office usually has variety in her job—phone calls, mail, record keeping, receptionist. Each hour she may be doing something different—achievement points. But if she works in a large office, she may spend all day at one detail; lacking variety in her work, the goal she may look forward to with keenest motivation is quitting time.

How variety in a job helps was demonstrated with the clerks in the offices of a large corporation. Dr. Nancy C. Morse divided the clerical jobs into two classes. One class provided variety in duties during the day, the other class lacked variety. The variety in these cases was not actually much, not nearly as much as in the one-girl office. But what little variety there was produced the following effects on the clerks' morale (94):

	Per cent of workers having high satisfaction with their jobs
On jobs providing variety	41
On jobs lacking variety	8

Note that about five times as many on the jobs providing variety had high morale about their work.

Do many workers in offices where routines are standardized feel dissatisfied over the lack of variety in their operations during the day? This is what Dr. Morse found for the same firm:

	Per cent
Dissatisfied because work lacks variety	23
Felt their work does provide some variety	27
Did not mention variety one way or the other ...	50

Assembly-line work is usually low in variety. In a modern automobile plant, one-third of the assemblers did only one operation. Another one-third did two to five operations, such as put four screws on a baffle, then insert nine clips—a two-operation job. The remaining one-third had jobs with five or more operations. The men doing fewest operations generally reported their work as least interesting. Drs. C. R. Walker and R. H. Guest also report that there was more absenteeism among the men who were working on jobs which had the extreme features of mass production (126).

Factors affecting variety

We have all noticed that one person doing a certain job will think it lacks variety, while another at the same work thinks it has variety. There are differences in people, as well as in jobs. As a rule, the less capable worker can be expected to think that a simple job provides variety. The less capable worker probably has lower goals, and the routine job reaches a goal for him, while it would not for a skilled machinist. This is one "higher" function the boss has to consider in assigning workers to jobs.

The style of the boss is also a factor in whether or not a job seems to have variety. When workers are allowed to move around, talk at work, take coffee breaks, a job seems to have more variety than it might otherwise. But when a boss supervises closely, a job with actually varied tasks may seem as if it were getting nowhere (58).

In an effort to be more efficient mechanically, there has been much simplification of work and of jobs. Work simplification means cutting out unnecesary details. This may not affect the variety of operations that are grouped together to provide a job for one worker.

Job simplification, in contrast, reduces the operations a worker does, making the worker more of a specialist, or routine operator.

A little variety can often be added to jobs that have been oversimplified. Girls assembling radios, for instance, had been soldering only six connections. Increasing the number of joints each girl soldered upgraded the work because it added some variety (127).

Work becomes more meaningful, and more goal-directed, when a job has variety. But not so much variety that it overtaxes the individual's abilities.

Giving prestige to the bricklayers' job

A goal which practically all work groups want to reach is to move upward by improving their job status, or prestige. Individual workers, too, are lured by the goal of winning a little more distinction for their jobs. They want—both groups and individuals—favorable recognition from their fellow workers, and from the community at large.

The leader who has good empathy will sense some of the "higher" things he can do to help his crew make headway toward more prestige (66, Chapters 12, 13).

One way is to keep workers centered on the importance of the job they are doing. This was illustrated in experiments for the Office of Naval Research, by Dr. Harold H. Kelley. He worked with people at the job of making artistic patterns with bricks (62).

Each of the 99 people he tested did exactly the same work. But some were told, "You have the best and most important job in the group." The remainder were told that the best jobs had been given to the others.

This chartoon visualizes the great differences made by those comments from the boss. The workers who were given the impression they had a low-class job expressed discontent about their work three times as much as the others.

In addition (not charted), those who thought they had the low-class jobs talked more about topics that were not related to the work. This is an example of trying to avoid thinking about topics that cause anxiety.

Another significant difference was that those on the so-called low-class jobs were more confused about how to do the work, although they turned out the same quality as the others. Apparently the job seemed harder because of the anxiety over their status. Hostility may also have helped cause this confusion; we recall that hostility toward the boss (for giving them a low-status job, in this case) often caused mental blocking so workers did not understand his instructions (page 12).

There was also an interesting difference in the interactions between the "high-class" and "low-class" workers. The ones on the low-status jobs talked more to the people on the high-

Words changed a low-class job into a high-class job

Discontent
with the job ·

(Much)

1.12

(Little)   .35

Told job was   Told job was
HIGH class   LOW class

class jobs, shunning those who were on low-status work. Talking to the higher-status workers added a bit of luster to the imagined low-class work. Research for the National Institute of Mental Health, and also for the Office of Naval Research, has revealed that people are inclined to talk more to those they think have higher prestige. This is considered a way to add a bit to one's own prestige feelings (13, 50, 119).

The grapevine, seniority, and other effects of striving for prestige

In the demonstration charted, about one-third of the artistic bricklayers were women. Ideas about job status had about the same effects on them as on the men.

Another illustration of the striving for prestige as a psychological and social force, is the direction in which grapevine rumors spread. Such rumors were fully traced in one office, and it was found they were spread to a person above by 65 per cent of the people, but to those below by only 12 per cent (6).

The boss who teaches his workers new job details is also upgrading the worker's status. Among railroad laborers, the bosses who trained their men for new duties had the higher-producing crews (59).

Skilled workers almost always enjoy greater prestige, off the job as well as on the job. This is a factor which makes skilled workers usually much more satisfied with their jobs, as well as with the company in general. They have made headway in winning recognition from others (60).

Many squabbles about seniority spring from concern about job prestige.

When workers can take part in planning job changes and other work details, their feeling of having status rises. They are thus helped to reach one goal, and, at the same time, they are setting up other goals to motivate them further.

The cliques helped their members make headway in this plastics firm

One of the "higher" functions which workers expect from their boss is for him to keep them informed about what is going on in the organization—above them and in other departments. Such background information makes jobs more meaningful, and lets the workers see how they fit into the whole picture. Workers can be helped to reach their goals, as well as set up suitable goals, if they are kept informed about what is going on that may affect their work, or goals.

Harold F. Smiddy, vice-president of the General Electric Co., pointed out at a meeting of the National Office Management Association, that workers' need for information about their part in the total effort has probably increased in recent years. Operations have become more technical, more specialized. The worker who is not brought up to date about how his work fits into the company as a whole, may merely go through the motions of his job, rather than work with initiative to reach a job goal.

Also consider that when the leader does not pass along inside information to his crew, they tend to seek it for themselves. This is where the grapevine, and cliques of workers, come into action.

The cliques in the home office of a plastics firm were analyzed over a two-year period by Dr. Edward Gross, for the Human Resources Research Institute of the U.S. Air Force. Dr. Gross found that the cliques were small, including only three or four persons on the average. But one-third of the office workers were in one clique or another.

He found that the members of the cliques were never competitors with each other. They had no anxieties about their prestige status when they were together. They felt at ease with each other, and trusted each other.

The members of any clique almost always came from different lines in the organization—sales, accounting, and other departments. A clique thus gave a cross section that cut across channels, not a sample from the same department or office. The cliques short-circuited the usual lines of communication from one department to another.

The main activity of the cliques was to get together and talk to each other—at the water cooler, during work breaks, etc. Much of their talk was about the work in their own sections. It was seldom gossipy. Almost always their talk was shop talk which kept them better informed about what was going on in the office as a whole. This inside information helped them guess executive decisions which might affect the goals they were trying to reach (39, 40).

These engineering executives spent most time on human-relations problems

This pattern of passing information across the lines also takes place extensively at executive levels, although cliques may not be involved. Dr. Tom Burns found this in a study of the top executives of a producing department in a British engineering firm. For a five-week period, all the communications of the top executives were recorded—mail, memos, face-to-face talks, telephone talk, luncheon talk, and so on (16).

Most of this shop talk of these executives was across the

lines, not up and down a line of control as an organization chart might lead us to presume it would go.

It is also revealing that these engineering executives had assumed that they spent most of their time on engineering and production problems. But the records showed they were in fact spending more time on human-relations problems that revolved around the personnel.

People doing specialized work seem especially to want to swap information across the prescribed channels. This may be just as well. When a job is simplified or specialized, it usually loses much of its meaning, and the workers' goals may become little more than wild hopes.

But when the leader keeps his group informed about company affairs that may have a bearing on their work, the goals workers hope to reach can be developed on a more reasonable basis. Their goals can be formed more on the basis that worker and employer have some problems in common, and the goals the workers are motivated to reach will likely be more mutually desirable.

In a large power company it was found that 47 per cent of the bosses of high-morale departments kept the men informed about what was happening elsewhere in the company. But only 11 per cent of the bosses of the low-morale departments passed along such information (57).

Face-to-face information helps make headway

Bulletin boards, memos, and the company newspaper are often used to pass information to the workers. These methods are not considered as effective as getting the information right from the lips of the immediate leader. Work groups expect this information from their leaders, as one of the "higher" functions the leader is supposed to perform for the good of his group.

Drs. H. J. Leavitt and R. A. H. Mueller have found that people catch the idea better when communications are made face to face, and they can ask questions as well as listen (71).

People have also been found by Dr. E. W. Bovard, Jr., to like their groups better when they can ask as well as listen. This is another advantage from the face-to-face method, and is likely one thing that makes cliques hold together strongly (14).

Keeping workers informed also includes letting the group, and individuals, too, know how well they are doing to reach the goals. At that power company just mentioned, 47 per cent of the bosses of high-morale departments kept the men posted on how well they were doing. But only 12 per cent of the bosses of low-morale departments let their men know how they were coming up to what the group or the company expected (57).

In the same company, 14 per cent of the supervisors were looked upon by management as being immediately promotable, 19 per cent as questionable or unsatisfactory (87).

Of the immediately promotable, 79 per cent of their workers said the boss kept them informed of what he thought of their work. But only 42 per cent of the workers under the *un*promotable said they were informed about how they were doing.

That does not mean that the promotable bosses criticized their workers. Quite the opposite. Only 18 per cent of the workers under promotable bosses reported criticism, but 40 per cent did who were under the bosses who had the cellar positions.

This passing along of information about how well goals are being reached is one of the leader's functions as a problem solver for his team. Although followers expect to have a hand in solving some of their close-at-hand work problems, they also expect their leader to be a "Great White Father" who can —and does—solve some of the "higher" problems over which workers feel that they themselves have little control. Experiments with infantry rifle squads, by Dr. F. Loyal Greer, now of the Institute for Research in Human Relations, stress that the more the leader is seen as a problem solver for the team, the more the followers try to follow him (37).

What the followers should say

Here are some responses to leaders' actions which show that the boss is living up to expectations in helping the team reach their goals:

"Our boss shows us why our work is important."
"He gives us work we can do best."
"He tips us off about what's going on."
"Our boss helps us avoid mistakes."
"He explains our jobs clearly."

"I know what the boss expects of me."
"The boss goes to bat for us, and gets results."
"He tells us how our work lines up."
"He gives us more interesting work when he can."
"He trains us for better jobs."

"We can count on him to look out for us."
"I know what my boss thinks of my work."
"He sees that we have tools and supplies when we need them."
"He gives us recognition for good work."
"He tells superiors about good work."

"He is reasonable about what he expects from us."
"He spends more time supervising than in production with us."
"We feel he is pulling for us, so we don't worry much."
"He is good at grooming men for promotion."
"He is good at helping us solve job problems."

"Our leader is a hard worker."
"Our chief seems proud of the crew."
"The boss keeps us encouraged."
"He doesn't overload us with work at one time."
"The company gives him authority to do the things he thinks should be done."

A recheck on that list will show that a large share of those activities depend not only upon the immediate boss, but also upon the style of his chief, and upon company policies. The boss who has his hands tied will not usually be regarded by his workers as being a leader who can help them make headway in reaching their goals.

Now we will progress to the topic of developing cooperative teams.

7 *Developing cooperative teams*

There are many places in modern business where high output, or useful ideas, cannot be credited to any one person. The productivity of an individual is often interlocked with the efficiency of the crew he works with. Such instances seem to be on the increase.

We will first look into some offices where output depended upon the team, not on an individual wizard. We will find that the workers themselves placed a high value on being with congenial teammates, and that the congenial teams generally turned out more production.

A cohesive group is the phrase social scientists use to describe a group of people who are welded into an harmonious, efficient working team. Cohesiveness is looming as a significant objective for the leader.

We will compare cohesive and noncohesive groups engaged in similar work. The cohesive groups come out ahead in practically every comparison.

Then we will track down some of the forces which have proved effective for increasing cohesiveness and cooperativeness in a crew.

It will become apparent that there are some unchangeable

conditions in modern business which make it difficult always to have interactions between workers, and between workers and boss, which are essential to weld people into cooperative teams.

The office clerks valued cohesiveness more than their fringe benefits

"What do you like best about working for the company?" was asked of 742 office clerks of an eleven-billion-dollar firm. The majority said it was the hours. Second place went to the congenial people in their own work groups. The benefits (vacation, sick leave, insurance) ranked third place.

The bosses of these same clerks were asked, "What do your employees like best about working for the company?" Most of the bosses gave first place to the hours, just as the clerks had.

But the bosses had low empathy for the value the employees placed on congenial workers. Congenial fellow workers was given top priority by 22 per cent of the clerks, while only 2 per cent of the bosses thought the clerks would place it that high (94).

Practically all similar records, from other organizations, show that bosses seldom realize how high the interpersonal relations on the job count with the workers (68, 125).

The leader has a harmonizing function. He has a crowd of workers to transfer into a congenial team that works enthusiastically together for some goals the members share. A congenial crew is cohesive—what the unions talk about as solidarity.

Cohesiveness involves:

1. Being personally *attracted to the other people* in the group
2. Being *interested in what they are doing together*, and developing zeal for the tasks shared with them
3. Recognizing the *need for each other*, and coordinating efforts and interactions to reach common goals.

Let's see how that works out in practice.

Absenteeism, teamwork, and the style of leadership

It's logical to suspect that absenteeism should be related to cohesiveness. This hunch was confirmed by the absences from a metropolitan power and light company. Drs. Floyd C. Mann and Howard Baumgartel found that group spirit was one of the most influential factors associated with this absenteeism (84).

The chartoon shows that most of the men in the offices that had fewest absences felt their groups were good at sticking together. A similar relationship was also found for blue-collar workers in this firm, though it was not quite as marked as with the white-collar workers. Absences were fewer where the blue-collar men felt they were accepted by their work groups, and where more of them felt their crews had lots of team spirit.

The men's absence rate also depended upon the style of the immediate boss. The absence rate of women workers in this firm was not clearly related to any of the factors on which records were collected.

How the style of the boss affects teamwork was shown in a

large research and developmental laboratory. About half of
the workers, who were under a restrictive boss, were reluctant

*Fewest absences in offices where the group stuck
together for their goal activities*

Men saying "Our
group better than
others at sticking
together":

62%

21%

LOW absence
offices

HIGH absence
offices

to do the teamwork required. But their counterparts, under a
permissive leader, were much more likely to accept their teammates. Those with the permissive boss socialized more with

each other evenings, had lunch together more often, and talked over personal problems with each other more (88).

When group thinks are used, cohesiveness is usually increased.

Pride in output

A look at production will throw more light on the desirability of coordinating workers into a cohesive team. Records compiled by the staff of the Survey Research Center show, almost without exception, that when workers have pride in being with their particular work group, output is higher (58).

We can again use office clerks to illustrate this in detail. One reason for the higher output in the cohesive offices was the mutual assistance of the workers. When one caught up with her own work, she spontaneously helped others catch up with their work. Teamwork is helped by working for a common goal to keep up pride in the output of a work group.

The benefits the firm had instituted apparently had not added to cohesiveness—athletic and recreational facilities, for instance. The clerks in the low-output offices took more part in these activities. This may have helped spirit for the bowling team, but it didn't carry over to their production goals.

About the same showed up in use of the suggestion system.

Pride in the crew output was also not related to how well the workers liked the details of their work, nor to whether or not they felt their work was important, nor to whether or not they felt they were treated fairly by the firm, nor to their satisfaction with pay. The fringe benefits—paid vacations, free lunches, sick leave, insurance—had little to do with their teamwork.

All those things may be desirable in themselves. But in this firm they didn't add up to spell cohesiveness. The array of benefits did not give common goals for productivity.

What did count for building teamwork in these offices was the style of the boss. Most of the bosses in the high-output offices were employee-centered. They spent more time coordinating than doing production work themselves. They didn't boss closely.

Providing motives to cooperate

An example of one way the leader can intentionally make the situation favorable for teamwork was demonstrated in a study by Dr. Martin Grossack, of people working on a human-relations problem. There were ninety young women, all high-school graduates, working in teams of five persons. Their interactions were entirely by memos to and from each other (41).

These teams shared a common goal: To find a useful answer to a human-relations problem. Production was measured by quality.

Some of the members had been secretly told they would be rewarded for the quality of their own individual solutions—this induced *competitive motivation*. Other members were secretly told their reward would be based on the quality of the decision reached by their team—*cooperative motivation* induced.

Could these remarks influence their cooperativeness? Definitely yes, as this chartoon shows.

Was there a difference in the way they worked? Very much. The memos written by those with the induced cooperative motivation showed more cohesive feeling—"we," "us." Their memos were more relevant to the problem, and offered more real solutions. They made more effort to reach a uni-

More of them felt cooperative when told it was group work that counted

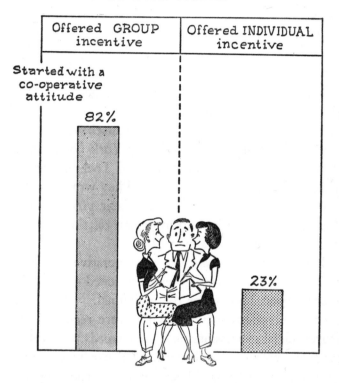

Offered GROUP incentive	Offered INDIVIDUAL incentive
Started with a co-operative attitude 82%	23%

form decision. They invited more interactions toward themselves. Their work was distinctly more cooperative, not every woman for herself.

It is worth noting, too, that those with the induced cooperative attitudes received more cooperation from others.

These spectacular gains in cohesiveness came almost instantly as the teams were formed. Gains might not be as quick, or as marked, with an established work team that had a tradition of rugged individualism.

For a similar experiment in the quick formation of cohesiveness among children, see reference (114).

Better relationships, working methods, and quality of work when cooperative motivation was touched off

Does such induced cooperative motivation work with men? And will it last longer than a few days?

This was tested by Dr. Morton Deutsch, of the Research Center for Human Relations of New York University, while he was at the Massachusetts Institute of Technology. He used fifty men, all high-school graduates. They worked in teams of five, once a week, for five weeks. Their goals were solving problems in mathematics and in human relations, which were workday concerns of the men (28).

Half of the men were given a cooperative briefing at the start. The remainder were given an induced outlook that emphasized personal glory for the individual.

Their interactions while at work were recorded in detail. Gestures, facial expressions, and their words were catalogued. After five weeks of squad work, a balance was struck to see what difference may have been caused by the cooperative or individualistic incentive used at the outset.

This chartoon shows how the cooperatively headed groups were far in the lead in group spirit.

Here are some other differences important to know about,

that are not on the chart. The men working with the induced cooperative attitude were far ahead in learning the names— and their correct spelling—of their teammates.

Better spirit shown by members of the cooperative groups

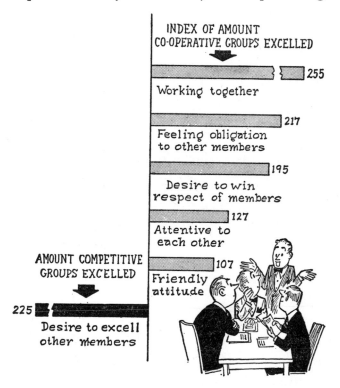

INDEX OF AMOUNT
CO-OPERATIVE GROUPS EXCELLED

255
Working together

217
Feeling obligation
to other members

195
Desire to win
respect of members

127
Attentive to
each other

107
Friendly
attitude

AMOUNT COMPETITIVE
GROUPS EXCELLED

225
Desire to excell
other members

These men were doing actual work in industrial relations. Did the cohesive squads reach better decisions? That is worth knowing, because their decisions might affect the fate of a firm.

The men on the cooperative squads produced decisions that were of much higher quality. Their gain in understanding the problems was also way ahead of the others.

How about working methods spontaneously adopted by the teams? The cooperative squads were superior in this regard, too. They organized themselves, and improved in effectiveness during the five weeks. But the squads of individualists worked haphazardly, and bogged down during the five weeks.

Here are other superiorities shown by the cooperative teams, given in index points, not percentages:

Coordinating efforts	259
Systematic and orderly work ...	197
Aware of where they were, and where they were headed	181

On two counts, however, the squads of individualists were ahead:

Difficulty getting ideas across ..	166
Desire to excel others on team ..	225

Six steps in building team spirit

Now for a classic demonstration of the social and psychological forces which can build group cohesiveness. A group that lacked cohesiveness was transformed into a highly cooperative team within a few days.

The team spirit became so rambunctious, in fact, that the teams shortly had to be broken up.

This quick building of cohesiveness was not done by asking for teamwork. No platitudes about cooperation, or slogans about one big family. No posters picturing the one weak link in the chain. The scientists just touched off the natural forces which are available when people are in groups.

This demonstration was made with twelve-year-old boys, in a secluded camp provided by the Yale department of psychology. The boys did not realize they were part of an experiment in human relations. The man they thought was the caretaker, for instance, was Dr. Muzafer Sherif, the chief psychologist (109, Chapters 9, 10; see also 110).

Here is an outline of the procedures by which the random collection of boys was built almost overnight into highly cohesive groups.

I. *Propinquity*. The boys were strangers to each other at the start. After they had been in camp a few days, they were divided into two groups. Each group was in separate living quarters. This is similar to most business situations, where strangers are put together to work in a room separated from other work groups.

Being thrown together physically (propinquity) gave a chance for interactions which would not otherwise have taken place. Propinquity thus provides an entering wedge for building team spirit, for the department at least, though not necessarily for the entire organization, as we shall soon see.

II. *Sharing common goals*. These separated groups of boys proceeded to set goals for their respective groups. They decided on decorations and arrangement of their quarters; the boss (disguised as the caretaker) didn't interfere. The teams decided on other activities which appealed to their own group. Each group worked feverishly for high production on these decorations and activities. Most of their talk was about these goals, and ways of reaching them.

This part of their situation was a bit different from some businesses, where the major part of the activities may be decided by the boss. With these experimental groups, however, the members participated fully in deciding their shared activities. Social scientists believe that sharing in making decisions, and then working together to reach these shared goals, are prime factors in building cohesiveness.

But when the common goal, or predominant activity, is not in step with a member's strong inclinations, he is likely to be a laggard in cooperation. And he will probably get out of the group at the earliest opportunity—the group usually provides that opportunity for him (106).

III. *Setting up an organization and accepting leadership.* These boys had not worked together more than a few hours before they began to pool their efforts. They spontaneously organized duties within the groups. They noticed that some members were adept at special activities, so they made niches in their organization charts for these experts. They quickly divided the work, and defined the responsibilities of different members; each member soon understood what role he was expected to play in the group life.

These groups also quickly came to look to a few members to play "higher" roles in coordinating the others. Captains and lieutenants emerged, and group activities began to center around these. The groups set up their own social levels, or hierarchies of power within the group. But their accepted leaders were from within the group, not from outside it, such as the caretaker whom they all bossed.

That is not always the situation with business groups. The business organization has already been set up when a new member enters. The person the company designates as boss may not be the one the group would have designated.

Cohesiveness is considered at its peak when each member comes up to the group's expectations in performing the special duties they think he should for the good of the group. This is especially true in the case of the leader. The others look upon him as being more responsible than the others in helping make headway toward their common goals (52).

IV. *Developing group symbols.* The boys had scarcely agreed upon their accepted leaders before the members were clamoring for symbols to identify themselves as distinct groups. They invented nicknames, and some jargon for their activities. Industrial groups do this if they are cohesive, and the vocabulary of one department may sound like Greek to the department down the line. The boys also developed some "secrets"—as offices do through the grapevine, and as families do in "family jokes."

The boys' groups bought caps and T-shirts, in the colors they decided upon as distinctive symbols.

Kid stuff? We shouldn't be hasty. Adults seem to have much of this same kid stuff in them. Railroaders favor a certain style of work clothes which are trade-marks of their group. A house painter feels disloyal to his occupational group unless he works in painter's whites. The blue shirt and the white shirt are group symbols in the business hierarchy. The work clothes are part of the role that members are expected to play.

Cliques within a department commonly settle upon some feature of dress as a badge of their clique—and cliques are strongly cohesive. In a department of one firm, the clique at the north side of the room (propinquity) dressed well, and ate expensive candy at work. The rival clique at the south side of the same room dressed sloppily, and ate penny candy. The members of both cliques received the same pay (66, Chapter 23).

When groups want such distinctive symbols, it is evidence of cohesiveness. But it does not necessarily follow that wearing a work uniform designed by the general manager's wife will build cohesiveness.

For a breath-taking account of how such symbols, and other factors, were used to build intense cohesiveness in the famous Carlson's Raiders of the U.S. Marine Corps, see reference (12).

V. *Competing with "natural enemies."* The situation with these boys was such that each group quickly looked upon the other as a "natural enemy." Groups tend to hold together more firmly when threatened by some enemy, or when some stress makes the members realize they are dependent upon cooperation for security or perhaps actual survival (38, 67, 130).

Rivalry and stress situations are not rare within a business. One department often looks upon another as a "natural enemy." The well-dressed clique considers the sloppily dressed clique as a rival; and each clique then holds together more strongly than before, and cooperates less and feuds more with the rival clique. In case the appointed leader is dogmatic and self-centered, the workers may become more cohesive—but rally around the goal of frustrating the boss rather than cooperating with him.

Business also has natural enemies outside the company walls.

These have been useful for intensifying cohesiveness in the business group as a whole, not just in a clique. Companies competing for the same business have been good rallying symbols for increasing cohesiveness (66, Chapter 24).

In the case of these boys' groups, the natural rivalry was exploited by egging the two groups into competitive contests. Little encouragement was needed; each group was itching to prove its superiority.

To intensify this rivalry, the experimenters rigged some of the contests. This made the losers furious—at their opponents. Each group held closer together than ever, and engaged in open as well as secret warfare. There were pitched battles in which the boy who had previously been the crybaby became an overnight hero of his group, but a despised villain to the other group.

To protect life and limb, it became necessary for the experimenters to order the hostilities stopped. Merely giving the order and policing the groups was not adequate.

More small-boy stuff? It reads quite a bit like Carlson's Raiders. Or like a brief history of some jurisdictional dispute.

It is clear that the competitive element in building cohesiveness has to be handled with asbestos gloves. Californians would probably not be as cohesive if it were not for the stimulating effect of the Florida chambers of commerce. But it is not as entertaining to think that perhaps the U.S.A. would not be as cohesive if it were not for the U.S.S.R.

VI. *Liking the people in the group.* Many social psychologists put this item near the top of the list for usefulness in building cohesiveness. One reason we are taking it up later is because the employment interviewer cannot pick and choose only agreeable personalities. Another reason is shown by this chartoon, which is based on the experiment with the boys' groups we have been describing.

Joining the groups, and working toward common goals, made more of them "Best Friends"

Choices received as "Best Friend":

91%

35%

BEFORE groups were formed

5 days AFTER groups were formed

This chartoon shows how much the other members' attractiveness increased *after* the group had been formed and had decided upon common goals. When the group was first formed, only 35 per cent of the boys in it were "best friends" with each other. But after a mere five days this was more than doubled. Many former second-choice acquaintances had become best friends as cohesiveness increased.

The opposite happened, too. The boys they had previously looked upon as best friends, but who had been put into the rival group, were now mere acquaintances, if not out-and-out enemies. Apparently friendships were determined to an extent by the groups to which they felt drawn.

That emphasizes the reciprocal relationship between cohesiveness and attraction to the people in the group. Cohesiveness seems to be built easiest when the people are mutually attractive to begin with. But as cohesiveness does develop, people who have not previously seemed attractive become so, if they are in our group. The people in "our group" usually seem (to us) to be a little more capable as well as more attractive than their counterparts in competing groups.

The preceding paragraph has some limitations which need explaining. Social forces do not work out that way in case an individual or two in the group do not sincerely accept the group's goals and ideals, and do not do their expected share in helping reach the common goals. In case an individual doesn't fall in step and play his expected role, the group looks upon him as a deviate, and is likely to consider him odd, or repulsive. The standardization of the group's ideas, or goals, is helped along by the rejection, or withdrawal, of any deviates who can't go along wholeheartedly with the others (5, 32, 106).

Presumably cohesiveness can be established easiest when the people in the team are aware of their likenesses, rather than differences, at the outset. Some experimental work has shown that simply telling people they were like-minded helped the cohesiveness of new groups that were being formed (33).

Conditions that encourage favorable interactions

In most of the examples in this chapter there is a common thread of interaction. Cohesiveness is built largely through interactions. When the conditions are such that the interactions are difficult, or hostile, we should expect cohesiveness to remain low. That is one result when the boss is restrictive and prevents interactions between his workers (88).

Another example is assigning workers to help each other. In a series of large offices doing similar work, 52 per cent of the clerks willingly gave help to other clerks whenever it was needed. These willing cooperators were mostly in the offices where high pride was shown in their output (94).

But in the same series of offices, it was the boss who decided who helped whom in 43 per cent of the instances. There was generally higher pride in productivity, however, in the offices where the clerks could pick their own assistance. Freedom to choose one's helper was apparently a part of the human climate that encouraged cohesiveness and the related pride in output.

The physical conditions of the work place may also put a wet blanket on interactions. Work in noisy locations is looked upon as unfavorable to cohesiveness. The noise makes it difficult to talk, and cuts down this interaction through which people develop cohesiveness. Some concern has been expressed about the trend to automation because it makes work places noisier.

Assembly-line jobs are also regarded as unfavorable for developing the spirit of teamwork, although the operations are highly coordinated by the conveyer. But the operatives are not coordinated in their interactions. The pace of the line keeps workers close to their assigned stations. About the only time there can be interactions is when the line breaks down. The assembly-line worker's cohesiveness may be more for the car pool in which he rides to work than for the workers in his immediate job circle (126).

Merely being together under the same roof will not of itself make a group cohesive, though it does provide propinquity as a starter.

A way to check the leader's methods

Here is a list of responses to procedures used by leaders which show how the leaders are playing the expected part in coordinating their followers into cohesive teams:

"Our boss knows what each of us is good at."
"He lets us help each other out."
"He is fair and does not play favorites."
"He gives us a chance to plan things."
"He keeps us posted about what our competitors are up to."

"He tries to put us with people we like."
"Our leader delegates authority wisely."
"He has a knack for knowing how we feel about things."
"He'll stick his neck out for us."
"He sees that the right people are put on a job."

"He is good at coordinating the different jobs."
"He is willing to cooperate with us."
"The boss has meetings with us frequently."
"He does not help us unnecessarily."
"He asks for our opinions about things."

"He tries to get favors for the entire crew."
"He gets us extra help when we need it."
"It's O.K. with him if we kid and talk on the job."
"Our boss seems to like all of the gang."
"He helps us work out things together."

Let's summarize briefly the leader's functions which have been presented to this point:

1. Setting goals WITH the group—including group thinks
2. Helping the team reach their goals, or make headway
3. Developing cooperative teams, or cohesive crews

The next cardinal function of personal leadership which we shall take up is "Helping them fit into the team."

8   *Helping them fit into the team*

Successful leaders have been found to have few black sheep among their followers. One of the leader's functions appears to be to understand the barriers which a group secretly agrees new members must pass if they are to be accepted as "one of us."

As we look into the records, we will find that about one out of five workers felt walled off from the team. This isolation was seldom due to what is commonly called personality. The rejection usually came because the worker neglected to conform to the customs or opinions which the team felt were important.

We will also find that differences in social status, and in skill, may cause a crew to give some members the cold-shoulder treatment.

Other studies to be summarized show how the size and location of the team are factors in isolation and rejection of some members. Also, that the three-person team may be most vulnerable on these counts.

Sociometric groupings of workers will be outlined, and records will be presented showing gains this new leadership procedure has brought in some work teams.

The use of cues in spotting potential sources of trouble will be presented. Throughout, you will notice the need for the leader, or boss, to reduce anxiety both in the group and in the new man who doesn't seem to fit in at first.

Workers who feel isolated

Workers spend more of their waking hours with their work group than with any other single group. That's a lot of propinquity.

One result of this seems to be a stronger feeling of affiliation toward the work group than toward the neighborhood group. This is reflected in tests on the sale of U.S. Treasury bonds. A larger share of people bought bonds when a fellow worker asked them than when a neighbor did. This is one of several indications that modern folks are more wrapped up in their work groups than in many other groups (75).

This chartoon shows, however, that a sizable share of 2,000 blue-collar workers in one modern factory felt that they were not accepted by the others in their work group. Drs. Daniel Katz and Robert L. Kahn reported that about half of these workers felt accepted. About one out of five was certain, or had qualms, that their work group did not include them (60).

These one-out-of-five individuals were isolates. Isolates usually have considerable anxiety over being kept on the outside looking in. The presence of isolates has many consequences for a work team, as the following summary of the findings for this factory indicate.

More of the men in the high-output groups felt they were really accepted by the work team.

About twice as many who felt accepted had high satisfaction with their jobs.

High satisfaction with the tractor firm itself was shown by 45 per cent of those who felt accepted, as against only 30 per cent of the isolates.

Only half of the workers felt they were really a part of the work group

In a power company, absenteeism was least among the workers who felt they were accepted by the others on their crew (84).

The leader and isolates on his team

Where do such facts lead us? The satisfaction from being accepted by the team reduces anxiety, and seems to spill over. It gives both the job and the company bigger halos.

Social psychologists doubt if satisfaction overflows in the other direction. This means that pride in the company would not be likely to give a worker satisfaction with his job if he felt he was spurned by his crew. Apparently company spirit can be built better from the bottom upward, using the work team as the unit with which to build cohesiveness.

Such considerations put a finger on the need to transform isolates into accepted team members. It may be more important now for the leader to attend to this function than it was in the recent past. Dr. David Riesman has summarized the changes in modern life which seem to have made group belongingness a stronger motivating force than in previous generations (101).

The immediate boss is probably more effective as a leader if the workers look upon him as belonging as much to the team as he does to management. When the immediate boss is accepted as "one of us" he is in a better position to fit all the others into a work team (90, pages 207–224).

The boss who is production centered may have many isolates on his crew without realizing it. But the worker who is kept at arm's length by the gang usually knows it. Experiments in the U.S. and in the Netherlands have shown that individuals who have unstable relations have a more accurate knowledge of how they stand in relation to others (31).

What are some of the cues that tip off the worker—and his boss—that he is not fitting into the team?

Syntality—how groups preserve their personalities

Some of these cues come from the personality of the group. You may have noticed that groups have personalities of their own. Some teams are conscientious and proud of their high output, for instance, while other teams are reckless and chiselers.

Syntality is the term used for a group's personality. Each group tries to keep its syntality—or personality—pretty much the same, month after month. They do this by (a) giving preference to "our kind of people" in accepting new members, and (b) by putting pressure on the other kind to become "our kind" (21).

Groups express their syntality by making it difficult for anyone to be accepted unless he fits the pattern of what the group wants to be like. A group that wants to hold down production, will not accept an eager beaver who turns out top production.

In his analysis of 500 ongoing groups, Dr. John K. Hemphill found most of them were slow to accept newcomers (44):

	Percentage of all groups
Very difficult to join	65
Medium difficulty	27
Easy to join ("open doors")	8

Three-fourths of these 500 groups also had rigid customs and traditions they enforced—unwritten laws about what was expected from members who were accepted as "one of us."

Pressures the group puts on new members

These group pressures, or folkways, may put more pressure on workers than do the standard procedures which are written in the manuals. The boss with his ear to the ground, or who came up through the ranks, may be aware of these unwritten crew-ways. He can tip off new employees to the rules which are not in the rule book, or get a pacemaker the crew accepts to take the newcomer under his wing (102).

"Knowing the ropes" usually means understanding some of these crew-ways which are used to preserve the syntality of a particular team.

Cues as to how the individual is fitting into the group come from the pressures the group puts on him. These pressures are the group's way of trying to get the new man to conform to their syntality. They may ignore him in their shop talk, pass difficult or dirty jobs on to him, make him the victim of unpleasant jokes, tamper with his machine or output, keep aloof from him during lunch or rest periods. Such pressures increase the isolate's anxiety.

The grapevine joins in pressuring. The isolate often becomes the subject of nasty rumors; he is a Communist, or his wife has an interesting past, they whisper (1, 2, 32).

The grapevine may also pressure the deviate, or isolate, by keeping useful news from him. In a leather-goods firm, Dr. Keith Davis found that 20 per cent of the executives were by-passed (isolated) when useful information went along the vine. It may not be an accident that that percentage is about the same as for the blue-collar workers in the chartoon. Executives, as well as bench workers, can become isolates (26, 27).

Conformists, deviates, and sliders

The highest hurdle to be cleared before one is accepted seems to be the group's opinions and beliefs. Syntality seems to demand like-mindedness even more than dressing alike.

They chose as best friend a person who had similar ideals

Degree the person matched the ideals:

67

6

NOT friends — ideals not matched

BEST friends — ideals matched

This was shown in the formation of friendships. Pairs of best friends were checked on a hundred different qualities by Dr. William R. Thompson. He also checked on how these people valued these qualities, or ideals, or goals (121).

The column on the left in this chartoon shows that the

pairs who were not friends scarcely matched in ideals, though they were of similar age, education, and social status.

The right-hand column shows the high relationship found between a person's own ideals and how he sized up his best friend as showing these same ideals.

Such records cast doubt on the assumption that a pleasant smile and a "pleasing personality" will do the trick of fitting a person into a group. Sharing ideals, or goals, apparently counts for considerably more than does personal glamour. The "charming person" is likely to be one who matches our ideals, and he may be far from charming to someone else.

Differences in opinions do matter in group life. A cohesive group strives mightily to keep all members thinking pretty much alike on topics the group considers important.

It works, too, at the neighborhood level. In one community, residents who conformed to the majority opinions of their neighbors were contrasted with residents who held different opinions [deviates]. Nearly twice as many of the conformists were chosen as "a person I would like to live beside" (32).

The importance of opinions over sheer personality in determining belongingness was also shown in experiments in which paid stooges deliberately shifted their opinions. Each stooge took part in several groups. In some groups the stooges consistently expressed opinions contrary to the majority [deviates]. In other groups they agreed with the majority [conformists]. And in still other groups they started out as deviates, but shifted to become conformists [sliders] (106).

These stooges were the same men, the same personalities, in each group. Yet when they played the role of deviates they were blackballed in elections. When they played the role of conformists the group placed them higher up the totem pole.

And as sliders, the groups tended to forgive their earlier errors of opinion.

Cues given the checkerboard girls

We have learned about some cues the leader can get from a group's behavior, and from a newcomer's behavior, which forecast whether or not the team will look upon the newcomer as belonging.

Many experiments show that the leader can also *give cues* to the group, and to the newcomer, which open the door wider for the newcomer's initial acceptance. While the leader's cues can trigger more favorable interactions at the outset, it is not reasonable to expect these cues to dissolve barriers completely.

One example comes from the girls who worked in teams of three to make checkerboards. The girls, we recall, were not acquainted with each other when they first came to work. In one phase of the experiment, 25 of the girls were given this cue: "There is every reason to expect you to like the other girls, and for them to like you." Another 25 girls were given the opposite cue (107).

All the girls were high-school graduates, and much alike in age and background. They were told those "scientific lies" to find what effect might be produced on the acceptance of the girls into the work teams.

After the first shift of making checkerboards, the girls in whom a positive attitude toward acceptance had been induced, or cued, showed much more liking for their teammates. Compare the columns in this chartoon to note the difference the two kinds of cues made.

Can you make the workers glad to know each other?

COLD
introduction

WARM
introduction

"Warm" and "cold" cues

Similar work with men, by Dr. Harold H. Kelley, revealed that cues had a powerful initial influence on the men's acceptance, too. The same persons were introduced to some groups as "rather warm persons," to other groups as "rather cold persons." When the cue was "warm," the groups gained the impression that the selfsame man was more considerate, more informal, more sociable, more popular, more good-natured, more humane, and even that he had a better sense of humor (61).

Other work has shown that such cues as "polite," or "blunt" do not make much change in the impression. But the expectations aroused by "warm" or "cold" have been found by several studies to be highly influential. This suggests that the notions of "warm" or "cold" trigger feelings which are more central in human relations.

A "warm" cue seems to allay group anxiety and to stimulate interactions. When Dr. Kelley used "warm" introductions, 56 per cent of the group took part in the interactions. But when the "cold" label had been pinned on the newcomer, only 32 per cent took part.

The right cues can apparently make the climate more favorable for a greater ease of talking (interactions), which should help the new man get a favorable start toward fitting into the organization (syntality) of his team.

Special problems of three-person teams

We have seen that the absorption of a new worker into the team is likely to be smoothest when the climate encourages favorable interactions. There are also some mechanical factors, they can be called, which influence the manner in which the new person fits into a group.

In groups made up of only three persons, for instance, one is very likely to be isolated by the other two. Such teams were observed through one-way windows while at work, by Dr. Theodore M. Mills, in the Harvard Laboratory of Social Relations, under contract with the Human Resources Research Institute of the U.S. Air Force (91).

There were nearly 500 interactions between the typical team members within a half hour. On paper, there should have been an equal division of talk to and from each person. It didn't work out that way, however.

Most of the teams quickly divided into a twosome and a leftover person—like the eternal triangle.

Other experiments confirm this tendency for a three-person team to give one member the mother-in-law treatment, and imply that three-person work teams may be an organizational hazard.

Environmental factors in acceptability

Where the person sits has also been found to influence the interactions, and his final acceptance. We might expect people to have most interactions when they sit beside one another. But what worked out was that there was a larger share of interactions with the person sitting opposite. This difference, Dr. Bernard Steinzor reports, may be due to the greater ease of getting cues from facial expressions when sitting face to face rather than cheek to cheek. Shrugs of the shoulders, and lifted eyebrows, often give meaningful cues (113).

The middle location was also found to be more favorable. In an assembly line of five to seven workers, for example, those in the middle locations usually receive and give most shop talk. The people at the end are relatively isolated.

Corner-of-the-room locations have also been observed to isolate the worker geographically in many cases.

A noisy environment, which prevents easy talking, may isolate a large share of a crew. So can a few dominating members who monopolize the interactions and touch off hostility in the others (108, Chapter 6).

Sociometric teams of house builders

Sociometric choice is a big phrase which means that each worker is asked, "Who is your first choice to work with? Your second choice?"

Every twenty-ninth house free, when workers chose teammates themselves

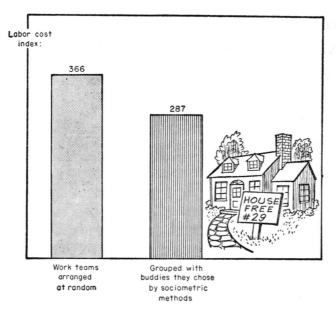

This chartoon shows some of the results when those simple sociometric choices were used to form teams of bricklayers and carpenters. All the workers were skilled, with many years of experience. They were building duplicate rows of houses in a large real estate development near Chicago (123, 124).

The boss had previously assigned teammates on a random basis, from the pool of available men. The column on the left shows the labor cost during the three months when the teams were just thrown together without regard for individual preferences.

For the next three months, Dr. Raymond H. Van Zelst used sociometric choices to form the teams. They were of the same workers, but regrouped sociometrically. The column on the right shows the significantly lower labor cost per unit when the men had, in effect, chosen their own work buddies.

There was also about a 6 per cent saving on materials used by the sociometric teams.

The contractor's chief engineer computed that the combined saving for the sociometric grouping was greater than any combination of five previous work-saving methods they had tried. He also reported: "We are now building every twenty-ninth house entirely free."

There were other gains after the workers had been regrouped. Job satisfaction went up considerably. Labor turnover went down.

Factors in sociometric teams of workers

Experiments by Drs. David Rosenthal and Charles N. Cofer have shown that it needed only one spiritless member to lower the morale of four- and five-man work teams (104).

There is evidence that some of the gains from sociometric groupings are partly due to the fact that workers have some say-so about those they work with. Considering the workers' wishes indicates a more democratic climate, which is a plus in addition to their being with other workers of their own choosing.

Dr. Fred E. Fiedler, for instance, has analyzed the relationship between output and attractiveness of other members in teams where the teams had not been formed on a sociometric basis. This work was done for the Office of Naval Research, with basketball and surveying teams (34, 35).

The basketball teams had been organized by the coaches on a basis of skill. The surveying gangs had been formed on a catch-as-catch-can basis.

No consistent relation was found between the degree of attractiveness within a crew and its output. In a few cases, in fact, there seemed to be a negative relationship.

One reason for lack of relationship in the basketball teams was differences in individual skill. This has business significance, too. It worked out this way: The players sometimes hesitated to pass the ball to the high scorer, "because he has all the glory already." By not passing him the ball, they were in effect rejecting, or isolating him. The high scorer was too good to fit into the group so far as the others were concerned; his superior skill touched off anxiety in the others.

Should the leader be a star maker?

This lack of cooperation with the most skilled players heads us right into the question of prestige status within a work group. Sometimes it is the best worker who is looked upon by the crews as being the misfit. We have earlier learned that 44 per cent of the clerks in one series of offices resented the high producers in their midst. The boss's pet usually receives ill will from the rest of the crew, too.

Groups whose members have uniform prestige and skill usually fit together better. Glory to the group, not to the high man, seems to be the feeling.

Differences in job status within a crew may also make it difficult to fit an harmonious team together. Those with high-status jobs tend to form a clique of their own, as do those on the low-status jobs—and the inspector gets the cold shoulder from both cliques.

Prestige for the group as a whole, however, is a different and more impelling force. It seems to be easier to feel pride in the accomplishment of one's group than of an exceptional individual in it. Teams on low-skill, or low-status jobs, are famous for their lack of cohesiveness.

The unwritten goal of uniformity within a team is also shown by the way members help out a low producer. When they cannot improve his job skills, they often pass some of their output over to him. This help is extended to the bottom men even when the others are on piece rate.

Groups incline to whittle down the superior, and to pull up the weaker. The presence of the superior worker triggers some anxiety; helping the weaker reduces the anxiety.

The leader's role can usually be strengthened if he helps along the weak member the group is trying to support, such as by training the weak worker in some special skill which the group sees is needed to help them make headway. That is another of the "higher" duties which most groups feel their leader should perform.

Unifying by separating

Occasionally the best way to solve a misfit problem is to separate the misfit from the group in a tactful fashion. One of the offices in the factory that was the subject of the first chartoon in this chapter was staffed mostly by young women, doing semiskilled work. There was one older woman among them who was at comptometer work. She did more skilled work and drew a bigger check than the others every Friday. That didn't help.

In addition, the older woman harped on the frivolousness of the younger women. During rest periods they chatted about dates and dances with an abandon intended to shock the spinster. Properly shocked, she tried to induce them to mend their ways. These pressures and counterpressures merely made the wall between them thicker.

The chief clerk did something before it was too late. He took over a small storeroom off the office. It had good light, and he told the spinster she could use it as her very own headquarters. Everybody was much happier from then on.

An example of unifying by separation, which reduced anxieties on all sides.

The right amount of anxiety

All these differences in belongingness point to the need for spadework by the leader to uncover cues and reduce anxieties from isolation. The isolate has anxiety over not being accepted. The group has anxiety over the isolate's threat to their uniformity.

A touch of anxiety is looked upon as inevitable in modern life, and as perhaps essential to motivation. But like rivalry and natural enemies, it can quickly become too much of a good thing (76, 116).

When the leader picks up cues that anxiety or hostility are on the rise, it is time to play a parental role—a cool, reassuring, encouraging role which reveals confidence in the future of the group as well as of the isolate. In short, interest in the group rather than self.

Is there much need for this unifying function in leadership? Membership in groups was reported as very pleasant in 50 per cent of the cases. Unpleasant was the verdict of 6 per cent. The remaining 44 per cent said neutral, or just so-so. These figures indicate there's still a job to be done with half of them (44).

How to tell if the leader is unifying his followers

Here are some ways workers describe the leader who is exercising his unifying functions to help them fit into the team:

"Our boss shows a personal interest in all of us."
"He is good at having the right people work together."
"He keeps us up to date on rules and regulations."
"He knows how we feel about things."
"Our boss teaches some of us new job skills."

"He got me started on the job right."
"We can see he is proud when we turn out a good job."
"He helps us when we need it."

"He is good at helping us solve personal problems."
"He considers our wishes when assigning work."

"He makes us feel at home in the group."
"He tips us off on how we can get along better."
"Our boss thinks about the same way we do about things."
"He doesn't play favorites.
"I don't worry so much after talking things over with him."

"He makes us proud of our team."
"He put me wise to the ropes when I first came here."
"He doesn't talk to us about 'touchy' subjects."
"He is usually pulling for the crew."
"He's all business, but we don't think of him as just a company man."

Now for a closer look at interest in the group rather than in self.

9 *Interest in the group . . . not self*

While the boss is wondering what to do about the worker who does not fit into the work group, it might occur to him that he, as a boss, also has a job of fitting himself to the group he is leading.

A look at the leaders of 500 groups scattered across the country will show us that the inferior leaders failed to fit into the groups they were supposed to be leading. The characteristic which was found most influential in making them second-rate as leaders was self-interest; they were likely to be more interested in feathering their own nests than in the goals or activities of their followers.

We will also see that bosses who were considered most promotable did not pull primarily either for themselves or for the company. The workers reported these promotable bosses as pulling for both the men *and* for the firm. Employees are quick to catch cues as to which way the boss pulls.

The first-line supervisor is in a critical position. He has to share, and to integrate, the goals of both the company and of the work team. This is a unifying function of leadership, and it raises a serious question about the wisdom of trying to make the first-line bosses primarily management men.

We will examine records that point out ways and means which the boss can follow to smooth out apparent conflicts of interest and integrate his crew into a company team. Let's start by taking a look at some bosses who failed to do that.

Failure in leadership from being self-centered

How many leaders strike their followers as being failures? A searching analysis, by Dr. John K. Hemphill, of 500 groups disclosed that 27 per cent of the leaders ranged from fair to downright bad (44).

Does top management have the same estimate? In a large electric power company, Drs. Floyd C. Mann and Howard Baumgartel found that top management sized up the first-line leaders as follows (87):

Questionable or unsatisfactory ..... 19 per cent
Immediately promotable .... 14 per cent

In this company, management and workers agreed fairly closely in spotting the inferior leaders. Both seemed to place a high value on the human-relations skills of the boss, as these figures show:

	Promotable bosses	Questionable bosses
Workers saying boss was good at handling people	71 per cent	27 per cent

That tendency is confirmed by the Hemphill reports. Of the seventy leadership procedures in which he checked the leaders, nine were uncovered which were almost exclusively characteristic of the failures.

Those nine most handicapping qualities of leadership are pictured in this chartoon. The most handicapping are on the left, with a slight drop in the handicap as you read from left to right.

Characteristics that helped most to make them inferior leaders

Other handicaps were found, which take up where the chartoon leaves off. The one at the top of this list was closest related to poor leadership, and there is a little less relationship with each succeeding characteristic.

	Per cent of all leaders
He was lax with the group	15
He couldn't be told anything	19
He boasted of his accomplishments	10
He flew off the handle	9
He let members get the best of him	5
He preferred the company of his superiors .	16
He reversed decisions once made	8
He apparently enjoyed ruling the roost ...	36

That list, and the chartoon descriptions, impress one with the predominance of human-relations items; selfish attitudes, particularly. The second-rate leaders gave the impression of being interested in their own success and prestige. The superior leaders showed more interest in the success and prestige of the group they were leading.

We will nail this down in more detail in the following capsule reports.

Successful leaders concentrate on the common interests

Where should the first-line boss's heart lie? With the group he leads? . . . With the company? . . . Or mostly with No. 1?

What happened in a going organization is shown in the Mann and Dent report. The pie in this chartoon is cut to picture the directions in which the employees said their bosses in this utility were pulling (87).

Dr. Hemphill got almost the same percentages in his study of 500 groups.

Did the direction the boss seemed to lean affect his leadership in this utility firm? Here's the answer:

	Per cent of promotable bosses	Per cent of questionable bosses
Pulled for the company	4	30
Pulled for both company and workers ..	75	40

How about the influence on productivity? Here's an answer from Dr. Nancy C. Morse's report on office workers in a large financial institution (94, page 157).

The direction the workers thought their bosses pulled

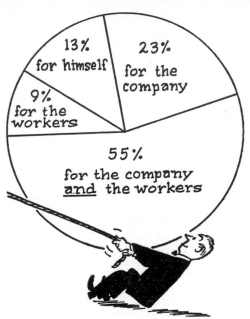

	Bosses' pride in high-output offices (per cent)
Pulled in direction of work group ..	58
Pulled about equally for company and workers	38
Identified by workers as primarily company men	13

A similar, but not as marked, relationship has been found in railroad laborers (59, page 19).

The biggest cut of pie in this chartoon shows that the first-line boss can integrate the goals of company and workers. It is not a question of divided loyalties, or of straddling the fence; rather, it is centering on the common interests of worker and management.

In short, to lead so that both workers and company **reach** their goals without getting in each other's way.

Cues that integrated common interests

Several laboratory-type reports have shown how the **leader** can unify groups by giving cues which emphasize integration. And that he can set a group-centered climate which helps integration better than a leader-centered (selfish) climate does.

One such demonstration is by Drs. Leon Festinger and John Thibaut, made for the Office of Naval Research, with groups ranging from six to fourteen persons. The experimenters measured the number of changes of opinions to reach a common agreement [integration of opinions] (33).

The people in thirty of the groups were given the cue that they were all much alike, and had about the same interests in the problems. The other thirty-one groups were given cues to emphasize the differences between members.

The people who had thus had their common interests rather than selfish interests cued, changed their opinions toward a common agreement 27 per cent more, on the average.

It was found that the cue of common interests had most effects on opinions on topics about which the people were not biased at the start. But there was still some unifying effect on their controversial opinions.

Those cues were given deliberately. But workers pick up cues from the boss, even when he does not intend to give any. The leader-centered style of boss, for instance, unwittingly gives cues which are much different from those given by the group-centered boss.

Those two styles were compared over a four-month period by Dr. Everett W. Bovard, Jr. Under the group-centered leadership the people became more friendly with each other, liked their groups better, talked more freely with each other, and became more alike in their judgments (14).

Those differences were not due to the leaders' inborn personalities. The leaders in that study were the same persons, who used group-centered methods with half of the groups, and leader-centered methods with the balance of the groups.

The relative unifying effect of the same two styles is compared in a widely used demonstration which was originated by Drs. Malcolm G. Preston and Roy K. Heintz. This shows how, under group-centered leadership, people come to a closer agreement with each other, and are better satisfied with the way the group finally comes to think about the problem (98).

Such unifying changes are due to the freer and more frequent interactions under group-centered conditions. In addition, hostility or anxiety is not touched off by the leader displaying an attitude of "I'm better than you are."

Going to bat for the followers

Another way the boss cues workers that he is not their natural enemy is by going to bat for them. Sometimes this takes courage, depending upon the attitudes of higher management.

The Hemphill records show that courage is one of the "higher" qualities that is related to successful leadership. Of the 500 leaders he tabulated:

	Per cent of leaders
Showed moral courage	56
Showed physical courage	32
Stuck their necks out for group ...	43

Each of those brands of courage had more bearing on the quality of leadership than did the boss's confidence in his decisions, or his ability to make decisions quickly. Apparently people follow a man of courage better than they do a man of decision, or a man of distinction.

How large a share of first-line supervisors have the courage to go to bat with management for their workers? In the offices of a large financial institution (58):

Bosses stand up very well for workers .... 36 per cent
Bosses stand up fairly well for workers ... 27 per cent

In an electric power firm (60):

	White-collar bosses	Blue-collar bosses
"My boss will go to bat, or stand up for me" .	72 per cent	58 per cent

Those figures indicate a considerable difference in the style of supervision between white-collar and blue-collar leaders in that firm.

An intensive study of 685 employees in the accounting department of this same power company was made by Mann and Dent. Most of these were white-collar workers, but one-fourth were meter readers and testers. About one-tenth were union members. The kind of courage a boss needed to go to bat about complaints was singled out for analysis. Forty-three per cent of the workers said their bosses did go to bat on their complaints (86, 87).

More of the promotable bosses went to bat for their
workers

But some of the bosses were more likely to do this than
others. This chartoon shows that the bosses who were most
promotable were also most likely to show this worker-centered courage.

How company policies have undermined personal leadership

That relationship can be expected to vary from company
to company. There is perhaps a small percentage of firms in

which higher management is on the defensive against complaints. This creates barriers against taking up complaints, and is likely to give workers the impression (or cue) that their boss stands between them and management.

In such circumstances, the situation is ripening for the work group to look toward some outsiders to give them the support they expect. That is where unions and stewards come into the act.

Another practical side to this worker-centered courage is whether or not the boss can make headway in adjusting complaints. We have already seen that Dr. Pelz found morale was lowered when the supervisor lacked power to get things adjusted, and that Dr. Jennings reported failure on this score when management took the power of adjusting complaints away from the foremen (55, 97).

Other work by Drs. Leslie J. Briggs and Robert M. Roe, for the Human Resources Research Center of the U.S. Air Force, showed that the morale of airmen in training was helped when they were actually encouraged to gripe (15).

But it is a horse of a different color if the leader joins in the griping. Hemphill found that one-third of his leaders did that, and that it gave no help to their leadership.

Born self-centered? Or cued to be that way?

This is the time to review some more material about the use of cues for triggering cooperation. Dr. Alexander Mintz has devised an ingenious bottleneck experiment which produced traffic jams whenever people in a group acted selfishly (92).

Each person held a string with a cone tied to the other end.

The cones were dropped into a large glass bottle. Then water was slowly let into the bottom of the bottle. The participants, who stood around the bottle, tried to fish their cones out before the rising water touched the cones.

Quick action was needed. Cooperation, too, because only one cone could be pulled through the bottleneck at a time. If several tried to pull out their cones regardless of the others, there was a cone jam—as happens when three cars try to get through a stop intersection at the same time.

In one set of trials, the people were cued by offers of individual rewards if they got their cones out dry. The column on the left of this chartoon shows that those groups produced traffic jams in three-fourths of their trials. When motivated to look out for No. 1, they pulled strings foolishly—"Me first" behavior.

But other groups were told it was a test of cooperative behavior, that there were to be no individual rewards. As the missing column on the right indicates, there was not a single traffic jam when the group had been cued for cooperation.

Dr. Mintz tried to cause traffic jams in the cooperatively cued groups by having accomplices shout and swear excitedly. But this device did not cause any jams.

He has also analyzed the influence of selfish cues upon the use of gasoline during the shortages early in World War II. The campaigns to cut gasoline consumption were not aimed at touching off cooperative behavior; nothing was said about using less gas for the good of the nation. Instead, selfish appeals—"So you can have your share"—and threats against chiselers were emphasized.

The records indicate that the simple announcement of the impending shortage cut down consumption slightly. But as soon as selfish cues were featured in propaganda, people apparently were triggered to get all the gasoline they could while the getting was good (93).

The "traffic jams" were all in the groups working for individual rewards

Such findings give grounds for believing that the cooperativeness of a group depends to a large extent upon the cues they have picked up, especially from their leaders. And people seem to read between the lines for cues, when the leaders do not intentionally give them cues for cooperative ways.

Cues the leader may give unintentionally

Does the boss himself seem to be a willing cooperator? This is one cue unintentionally given.

Dr. Hemphill found this was closely related to success as a leader, and was a characteristic of 87 per cent of the leaders he put under the microscope.

Dr. Martin M. Grossack found that cooperatively minded people were more likely to influence one another than were selfishly minded people. His cooperative people "just naturally" expected others to be more cooperative with them, and the others actually were more cooperative (41).

Unwitting cues also come from the way the boss delegates his authority. We have already seen what happened when management did not delegate enough power so that the first-line boss could handle complaints.

The Hemphill analysis revealed that 64 per cent of all his leaders delegated authority wisely. This delegation of authority had a close relationship to success as a leader, contributing more to his success than ability to explain things clearly, or trying to do a good job, or knowledge of technical details of the work.

Another cue, which may be an offshoot of delegating authority, is planning WITH the group rather than for them. In the Mann and Dent report, five times as many employees under the promotable bosses said that their boss frequently had group meetings with them. In addition, Mann and Baumgartel have found that absenteeism is less prevalent under bosses who use frequent group thinks (84).

Cues to help prestige feelings

A whole cluster of cues revolves around prestige. These are important in the U. S., but may not count for as much in countries which have a tradition of caste and class differences.

Although—or perhaps because—most Americans are hopeful about improving their status, they are unusually sensitive about being reminded that someone else is higher up the totem pole.

When cued that they are near the bottom of the heap, the common reaction is to prove that "I'm as good as you are" with some obstructive behavior. The opening chartoon of this chapter is filled with such unfavorable cues.

The boss who prefers the company of his superiors is giving his work group the cue that he is a social climber in the company. Or that he is turning his back on his crew. Hemphill found this characteristic of only 16 per cent of his leaders— and almost invariably these leaders were ranked as failures.

A related cue comes from the boss who seems to have plenty of time to spend with the crew. That is a favorable cue. It was given by 70 per cent of the Hemphill leaders.

But this cue depends not only upon the way the leader would like to lean, but also upon how much time he has available. Sometimes the firm loads him down with too much paper work and extra duties.

And sometimes the boss himself, if he is ambitious, takes on extra, or outside duties which drive a wedge between him and his work crew. In this case, the group may infer, and perhaps correctly, that the boss is more interested in his own advancement than in helping his crew make headway.

Cues bearing on favoritism

Favoritism is another cue bearing on prestige differences. Hemphill reported that 73 per cent of his bosses showed *no* favoritism. This was closely related to success in personal leadership.

Dr. Morse found that 27 per cent of the office clerks she analyzed felt that the way to get ahead in the company was to know the right people. Most of this 27 per cent who believed favoritism counted in promotion were dissatisfied with their own job prestige, or status. Apparently they wanted keenly to improve their status, and as a consequence were touchy about cues that suggested favoritism or office politics.

Being easy to talk to is another cue related to prestige differences. Hemphill found this characteristic of 85 per cent of his leaders, and that it was significantly related to successful leadership. Numerous other studies have reported that production and morale are higher when workers feel free to talk over personal as well as job problems with the boss, as well as to gripe to him.

We have previously seen that followers want their boss to be a little superior to them. But not *too* superior. Superior ability or skills may not handicap the boss, but airs of superiority quite likely do. A little difference in prestige goes a long way.

Prestige for the entire group

It is worth repeating that people in a group are touchy about prestige differences within the group, but that they do

want prestige for the group as a whole. When outsiders display favorable attitudes toward a group, it gives the members an extra measure of prestige they can all share; no favorites, and no rivalries touched off between the members.

A similar feeling of prestige for the group is cued by the boss's attitudes. Hemphill found that 76 per cent of his leaders were very proud of their groups—"the best crew of enamelers this side of hell." This attitude was significantly correlated with success as a leader.

The opposite attitude—where the leader boasts about himself rather than his group—was recorded for only 10 per cent. As you probably have guessed, this attitude was held chiefly by the failures among the leaders.

As the leader goes up the ladder, his followers will have different backgrounds and expectations from those of the group he started with. Then he can put on more airs of prestige, if he is so inclined. But only slightly more, else the new group of followers will get the cue that he is more interested in self-glory than in the purposes of the group.

From a company point of view, the common thread in all types of executive work is to maintain the organization as an organization—to unify company and workers of all levels so that they pull together toward the goals they have in common (9, Chapter 15).

What they say tells a great deal

The boss is giving his workers unifying cues when they say such things of him and his methods as:

"Our boss is proud of us."
"He pulls for both the company and for the crew."

"He goes out of his way to stand up for us."

"He is easy for us to see, without any runaround."

"He gives us all an even break."

"We don't think of him as mostly a company man."

"He talks over some of his work problems with us."

"He goes to bat for us."

"We have meetings with him to talk over the work."

"He can get things we need from the company."

"He does not interfere with our rights."

"He delegates responsibility wisely."

"He asks our opinions frequently."

"I feel that I know him well."

"He seems to enjoy being with us."

"I'm sure he believes in us."

Our next chapter will deal with the sixth essential general function of successful personal leadership, "human-ness" which helps the leader as a smoother-outer.

10 *"Human-ness" in the leader*

Many little books feature the belief that friendliness and a "pleasing personality" are the steppingstones to personal leadership. However, operational records of successful and unsuccessful leaders put friendliness and personality in a different perspective. Those "hello boy" characteristics have been found to be helpful, but they come out near the bottom of the list when actually tested.

When the slide rule is used on the records, it is found that the leader has six objectives to keep in view. Here they are, in the order of their bearing on success in personal leadership; the most significant is at the top, least significant at the bottom.

> Set goals WITH the crew
> Help them make headway toward those goals
> Coordinate the crew members
> Help individuals fit into the crew
> Interest in the group, not self
> "Human-ness"

We will review records which show that human-ness is a factor, though not the major one, in promotability, productivity, and morale. Human-ness is a bit different from the notion of the "nice guy" with a big smile and soft soap who strives to win others to him. Rather, it is a style of behavior toward others that keeps their hostile and anxious tendencies at a minimum.

The goal of human-ness in personal leadership is to improve the crew's performance and spirit by a style of leading which (a) does not touch off, and which (b) also allays latent hostile or anxious feelings in the crew.

The undercurrent of hostility in all human relations

Some hostile feelings are shown in most interpersonal relations, even at times in happily married couples. Another example is in the feelings people have when they are first introduced, which have been analyzed by Drs. John W. Thibaut and John Coules, with the aid of a grant from the graduate school of Boston University (120).

They introduced men to each other under standard circumstances which should not have aroused hostility. No cues were given to make the men think the newcomer might be "warm" or "cold." The men were all of about the same age, education, and social and occupational status.

This chartoon shows the mixture of feelings as the men sized up one another on this first meeting. Not quite half of these first feelings were friendly.

But notice, also, that almost one-third of the feelings were hostile. These were shown by imagining the other person had undesirable characteristics. He was criticized, secretly of course, for his clothes, or voice, or beliefs. Hostility was shown by tendencies to reject, resist, or oppose him.

Why this hostility? Nothing had been done during these

first fifteen minutes to arouse it. The hostile impulses were apparently just in the men, and cropped out in their interpersonal relations with a stranger.

The mixture of feelings when they first met each other

The leader needs to be aware of that undercurrent of "normal hostility" in our present world. The polite "Pleased to meet'cha" seldom tells the whole story. They may be 46 per cent pleased, but may also be 32 per cent hostile at the same time.

One of the leader's tasks is to keep the hostile tendencies from getting much above that "natural" 32 per cent. Too much hostility harms the team's cohesiveness, and interferes with making headway.

But some amount of hostility seems necessary for human motivation. A touch of hostility spurs people to action. So another task for the boss is to keep the supply from disappearing entirely so that conditions become just too "palsy-walsy." But there is rarely any need to worry about that.

Active, passive, and indirect hostility

Active hostility is easily spotted. It may be shown by threatening to fight. Or by breaking rules deliberately; by slow-downs and wastage; by swearing, arguing, criticizing. Such group actions as boycotts, strikes, and riots express active hostility.

Some vandalism and pilfering is caused by active hostility. Tampering with a "rate-buster's" machine is an example. Belittling nicknames, too.

Passive hostility may mislead the leader. The worker who keeps out of the boss's way often does this because of hostility. Passive hostility may make another worker apathetic and not interested in his work. Absenteeism and carelessness may indicate it. A large degree of misunderstanding instructions is an exhibition of passive hostility.

Alcohol may temporarily change passive hostility into active. The meek chap who avoided you now wants to fight you.

Stresses in the work situation may also change the passive

into active hostility. As when a change in work method is made autocratically. The pajama girls were an example of this.

Indirect hostility is shown in disguised ways which help the person keep his conscience clear. He can criticize the umpire, or watch fights on TV to express some of his hostility. Or he can pass along unfavorable rumors he thinks are "the gospel truth." Accident-proneness, in some cases, may be self-punishment for hostile feelings over which he inwardly feels guilty (66, Chapters 13, 14).

Anxiety about the hostility which others direct at us also enters the picture. More about that shortly (89).

The leaders' attitudes toward hostility shown them

"Don't run for office unless you have a thick skin," is common advice for political aspirants. Once elected, the dead cats begin to fly at the politician's head. Not only from the "outs," but also from some of the "ins" of his own party.

That advice goes for bosses, too. The position up the totem pole makes the leader a natural target for whatever hostile feelings people may have. This apparently undeserved show of hostility toward them unnerves a few individuals who become crew bosses. Some of them can't take the hostile pressures and they quit the job (76).

Some react with counterhostility; they threaten, push back, exercise discipline—the Bulldogs. They unwittingly feed back hostility which cues the men to push the boss with bigger doses of hostility. The Bulldog is sometimes merely fighting back at the hostility he should normally expect from a crew.

Then there are a few leaders who are so anxious over the

natural hostility their position draws that they lean over backward to be regular guys—the Fraidy Cats. They read books on how to be popular. An excessive fear of being disliked (anxiety) prompts these to do most things with a view toward helping their popularity. Minorities may run the department for them.

It usually doesn't work out as pathetically as with the Bulldogs or Fraidy Cats, because: (a) the people who come to be accepted as leaders have the capacity for taking hostility (thick-skinned) without feeding it back, and (b) they have a knack for handling people so that hostility is kept at the necessary minimum, or (c) they put the workers' hostility to work in reaching group goals, or against natural targets other than the boss, such as a competing firm.

This is borne out by Dr. Hemphill's analysis of the 500 leaders. He found that 91 per cent of the leaders were always or frequently friendly, despite any undercurrent of hostility in their crews. Eighty-five per cent seemed to like people in general, ignoring the hostility of people in general. And 48 per cent could make the team laugh—a good way to reduce their anxiety, if you can do it (44).

How successful leaders keep hostility low

The leader who can handle the hostility of others, and his own hostility, is on the more likable end of the scale. And a survey of power-company supervisors by Drs. Floyd C. Mann and James K. Dent showed that the likable ones predominated among those who were considered promotable (86).

The left side of this chartoon shows that 56 per cent of the workers under the promotable bosses thought they had a likable boss. A much smaller share of the blackballed bosses were liked by their workers.

This management was not running a popularity contest. It

A larger share of the promotable bosses were likable

was sizing up supervisors on all-around results, before promoting some of them into the big league. Those desirable results depended partly, as the chartoon illustrates, upon the likableness of the boss. It is easy to find reasons why the records came out that way.

The likable boss takes a personal interest in his workers, which allays their anxieties as well as making the boss less of a target for their hostility.

Output is almost always higher for the boss who has an interest in his employees as individuals. This interest in individual workers often helps their satisfaction, but not always, because it may increase ambitions. Of the 500 leaders, 77 per cent treated their followers as individuals (44, 58, 94).

The boss who helps his crew make headway toward its goals is thereby lessening their hostility. This makes him more likable to them, though it may not make him one speck more likable to his neighbors whom he does not help along.

The same goes for helping workers solve personal problems. This eases up some employee anxieties or worries. The workers like the boss more for it, but this may have nothing to do with how the boss's own children like him.

Such examples make the point, also, that human-ness is something more than lavish flattery and a glad hand, or trying to get good will with gifts and fringe benefits.

How successful leaders manifest human-ness

Human-ness is a sincere interest in helping the group make headway, combined with skill in handling the hostility and anxiety which seem to be inevitable in interpersonal relations.

Some ways in which Dr. Hemphill's blackballed bosses failed on this score were: more likely to be bossy, driving, and unreasonable. Those are common reactions against hostility that a person feels is directed at him. And they usually arouse counterhostility—the Bulldogs feed back the wrong cues.

Cues that trigger responses which are likely to keep hostility away from the task at hand are the essence of humanness. Here are some of these positive cues, and the percentages of Hemphill's 500 leaders who used them:

Positive cues	Percentage
Was friendly	91
Kept his word	86
Easy to talk to	85
Talked in a pleasing manner	85
Could be counted on in tough spots	81
Gave orders pleasantly	78
Was very proud of his crew	76
Remembered when person did a good job	74
Could take it when going was tough	71
Could appreciate joke on himself	62

Each of those ten cues had a positive bearing on success in personal leadership. They give a picture of a person who is himself apparently free from excess anxiety and hostility, and who is not so much concerned about winning friends that he can't tend to his business of helping the team make headway as a team.

Threats, criticism, discipline, and leadership

We have seen that the boss is in a poor position for winning a popularity contest. His job requires that he do many things which could arouse hostility, if done in the wrong way. Consider pointing out errors, or criticizing, as examples.

Those popularity-sapping duties can be done with a humanness, however, that can keep the boss from becoming a scapegoat. That was demonstrated by the 500 leaders, who came out with a greater popularity than would be expected in a random sampling of mankind. Yet these leaders didn't skimp on unpopular duties that needed doing. Apparently it is not

Less criticism reported by the employees of the promotable bosses

evading unpopular duties, but the human-ness of the way they are done that matters.

We can see how this works out if we put the microscope on that hostility arouser, criticism. Among the utility bosses, Mann and Dent found that four out of five employees under the most promotable bosses knew what the boss thought of their work. But only half as many knew who were under the bosses who couldn't squeak through as promotable.

But letting a man know what you think of his work does not mean that you have to use bare-knuckled criticism. Hasty criticism, in which the worker is given the old one-two, is a different breed of dead cat. The impatience that goes with the quick criticism shows hostility, which is likely to cue back hostility from the employee.

This chartoon shows how such quick criticism worked out for these utility bosses. Put this chartoon and the preceding paragraphs together. The promotable bosses were more likely to let a man know how his work rated. But these promotable bosses let him know with a human-ness which did not make it seem they were picking a bone with him, or rejecting him as a person.

Threatening employees with discipline, on the other hand, is a blood relative of quick criticism. A threatening boss is a hostile boss. Such threats have been found to go with low output (25, 59).

A test of blunt criticism

It's not news that blunt criticism cuts into friendliness. But it is useful to know how much it cuts. The Thibaut and Coules experiment, used for the opening chartoon of this chapter, also measured this.

One man in each pair they introduced was an undercover agent, a conspirator. After fifteen minutes of small talk, he bluntly criticized the innocent stranger. The index of friendliness toward the undercover agent was 46 before this criticism. It nose-dived to a low of 12 immediately after the un-expected criticism.

There was more comeback in friendliness, though, when the criticized person had a chance to talk back and answer the criticism right away. The nose dive was down to 7.5 for those not given a chance to talk back. It was only 17 for those who could talk back and get some of the aroused hostility out of their systems at once—an example of the usefulness of letting workers blow off some hostility without shushing them.

Here is a summary of ways the 500 leaders used positive cues when it was necessary to make criticisms:

Positive cues	Percentage
He listened to others	79
He could see both sides	75
He could make tactful criticism ...	56

Example of the Air Force crews

Which would you estimate counted more in producing output in a crew: The crew's friendliness toward each other? Or their friendliness earned by the boss?

These have been compared by Drs. Hans H. Strupp and Howard J. Hausman, aviation psychologists, in the Human Factors Operations Research Laboratories of the U.S. Air Force. They analyzed nine aircraft maintenance crews who worked in the same hangar (115).

The column on the right shows the significant relationship found between the output of a crew and the degree the members of the crew liked each other. The column on the left shows that the crewmen's liking for their chief counted significantly more in their high productivity. If the crewmen were shifted to another crew, and had to choose whether the crew chief rather than other crewmen went with them, they would probably want it to be the chief.

Productivity highest when aircraft mechanics were attracted to their chief and to other crew members

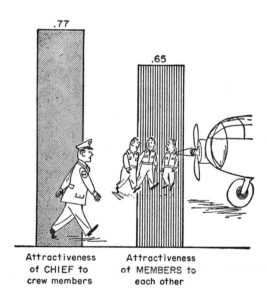

Correlation
with output:

.77

.65

Attractiveness
of CHIEF to
crew members

Attractiveness
of MEMBERS to
each other

This sociometric acceptance of the chief had a much higher bearing on crew morale than on productivity.

These crew chiefs had originally been appointed by the higher-ups, and the crewmen had no say-so in these original appointments. Yet some of the chiefs had more of the human-ness it takes to be accepted by the crew members as their leader. And when thus accepted, they were more effective as leaders, both in productivity and in morale.

How the feedback builds up human-ness

What human-ness made some of these chiefs more acceptable and more attractive to their crews? It was not that the chief was easy on the crew. There was also no consistent trend for the autocratic or democratic styles to be more accepted.

But it did help if the chief had a good idea of the technical skill of each man on his crew. The most attractive chiefs had the empathy to rule out their personal likes when assigning men to job details. They were less likely to play favorites, more likely to coordinate the work, so that the men felt they were making headway on their job goals.

That illustrates the endless chain in group forces. It is difficult to tell which single factor was the king link. It went something like this with these crews:

Some of these chiefs were doubtless a bit more agreeable than the others when they first reported for duty with the crew. Less "normal hostility" touched off at the start. That helped productivity a bit, morale a bit more.

As the crews became more smooth-running under the leader the men accepted, there was less feedback of hostility. The cues were for mutual acceptance, not for hostile rejection. This, in turn, boosted productivity and morale a bit.

This feeling of making still more headway fed back more acceptance for the chief. The crews began to feel some pride in their superior output, which would feed back to motivate them to keep up the record, perhaps better it. Because their accepted leader was playing the part they expected in this headway, some of the pride spilled over and polished his halo.

That sketches the high spots of the way acceptability is built up by the feedback of interactions. Note that it is not going around in the same old circle. It is more like an ascending spiral.

Example of the community leaders

A demonstration of the far-reaching effects of favorable feedbacks in an ascending spiral was made by Dr. Milton W. Horowitz, at the National Training Laboratory in Group Development. This was concerned with the way adults, who were leaders in their home communities, accepted or rejected others' controversial acts (46).

Dr. Horowitz found that when the reprehensible act was done by a person who had previously been rejected, it was roundly condemned—descending spiral. But if done by a person they had liked before the questionable conduct, it was likely to be either approved or condoned—the ascending spiral did not collapse.

This suggests that the boss who has to do some unpopular deeds in his line of duty will not suffer as much loss of acceptability if he has previously established a favorable feedback in his interpersonal relations with his followers (47).

It is also helpful for the leader to bear in mind other ways in which one feedback seems to cancel another. In the case of the aircraft mechanics, the relations with the chief counted more than the acceptability of other crew members. This was probably because groups look to their leader as the one person most responsible for the crews' making headway. When the chief had an acceptable personality to begin with, that gave an initial feedback which could neutralize some of the less acceptable duties he had to perform.

The big smile, glad hand, and pat on the back are, so to speak, fringe requirements for personal leadership. They can give some help for survival in the early stages of the rat race. But they don't take the place of the broader human-ness that can deal successfully with hostility and anxiety.

Try this on for size

In a capsule: The successful leader appears to be a person who gets things done *and* whose interpersonal relations with his crew are such that the members accept him as a person as well as a technical man.

What goes before and after that *and* are interlocked. Build up one side, and the other side gains.

Both sides probably need to be cultivated by the leader. Technical know-how for getting things done supplemented by the human-ness which builds personal acceptability. The leader can help balance these two by expecting hostility, and by not feeding it back to the crew.

After all, it is possible that a large part of the boss's pay check is for taking hostility and not minding it.

* * *

A leader is giving cues which feed back to build personal acceptability when his crew members say:

"Our boss seems to like everybody in general."
"He takes a personal interest in his men."

"He gives each of us the jobs we can do best."

"Our boss is a 'warm' sort of person."

"I wouldn't take another job unless my boss went with me."

"We like him better the longer we work with him."

"He seldom flies off the handle."

"He can make us laugh."

"He goes out of his way to help on our personal problems."

"He can take the gaff without getting flustered."

"He gives orders pleasantly."

"Our boss can take a joke on himself."

"He sticks to his word."

"He is friendly, not aloof."

"He talks in a pleasing manner."

"I feel at ease in talking with him."

"He is tactful when making criticisms."

"He can see both sides of a question."

"He is not much for arguing with us."

"He gives recognition for good work."

There are additional chartoons and brief discussions on topics related to the present book in our book, *Practical Business Psychology*, revised edition.

A composite picture of the methods of successful leaders

Sources referred to in the text

1. Allport, G. W.: *The Nature of Prejudice*, Addison-Wesley Publishing Company, Cambridge, Mass., 1954.
2. Allport, G. W., and L. Postman: *The Psychology of Rumor*, Henry Holt and Company, Inc., New York, 1947.
3. Arnold, T.: Report of the Assistant U.S. Attorney General, Government Printing Office, Washington, 1941.
4. Asch, S. E.: "Effects of Group Pressure upon the Modification and Distortion of Judgments," in H. Guetzkow, *Groups, Leadership and Men*, Carnegie Institute Press, Pittsburgh, Pa., 1951.
5. Back, K. W.: "Influence through Social Communication," *Journal of Abnormal & Social Psychology*, 1951, vol. 46, pp. 9–23.
6. Back, K. W., et al.: "The Methodology of Studying Rumor Transmission," *Human Relations*, 1950, vol. 3, pp. 307–312.
7. Bales, R. F., et al.: "Channels of Communication in Small Groups," *American Sociological Review*, 1951, vol. 16, pp. 461–468.
8. Bales, R. F., and F. L. Strodtbeck: "Phases in Group Problem-solving," *Journal of Abnormal & Social Psychology*, 1951, vol. 46, pp. 485–495.
9. Barnard, C. I.: *The Functions of the Executive*, Harvard University Press, Cambridge, Mass., 1947.
10. Bell, G. B., and H. E. Hall: "The Relationship between Leadership and Empathy," *Journal of Abnormal & Social Psychology*, 1954, vol. 49, pp. 156–157.
11. Berkowitz, L.: "Sharing Leadership in Small, Decision-making Groups, *Journal of Abnormal & Social Psychology*, 1953, vol. 48, pp. 231–238.
12. Blankfort, M.: *The Big Yankee*, Little, Brown & Company, Boston, 1947.
13. Blau, P. M.: "Interactions in a Government Agency," *Human Relations*, 1954, vol. 7, pp. 337–348.
14. Bovard, E. W., Jr.: "Group Structure and Perception," *Journal of Abnormal & Social Psychology*, 1951, vol. 46, pp. 398–405.

15. Briggs, L. J., and R. M. Roe: "Morale as a Function of Opportunity to Register Complaints," *Technical Report 53–4*, Human Resources Research Center, U.S. Air Force.

16. Burns, T.: "The Directions of Activity and Communication in a Departmental Executive Group," *Human Relations*, 1954, vol. 7, pp. 73–97.

17. Caplow, T.: *The Sociology of Work*, University of Minnesota Press, Minneapolis, Minn., 1954.

18. Carter, L., et al.: "The Behavior of Leaders and Other Group Members," *Journal of Abnormal & Social Psychology*, 1950, vol. 46, pp. 589–595.

19. Carter, L., et al.: "The Relation of Categorizations and Ratings in the Observation of Group Behavior," *Human Relations*, 1951, vol. 4, pp. 239–254.

20. Cartwright, D., and A. Zander: *Group Dynamics*, Row, Peterson & Company, Evanston, Ill., 1953.

21. Cattell, R. B.: "New Concepts for Measuring Leadership, in Terms of Syntality," *Human Relations*, 1951, vol. 4, pp. 161–184.

22. Chowdry, K., and T. M. Newcomb: "The Relative Abilities of Leaders and Non-Leaders to Estimate Opinions of Their Own Groups," *Journal of Abnormal & Social Psychology*, 1952, vol. 47, pp. 51–57.

23. Coch, L., and R. P. French, Jr.: "Overcoming Resistance to Change," *Human Relations*, 1948, vol. 1, pp. 512–532.

24. Collins, O., et al.: "Restriction of Output and Social Cleavage in Industry," *Applied Anthropology*, 1946, vol. 5, pp. 1–14.

25. Combs, A. W., and C. Taylor: "The Effect of the Perception of Mild Degrees of Threat on Performance," *Journal of Abnormal & Social Psycnology*, 1952, vol. 47, pp. 420–424.

26. Davis, K.: "Management Communication and the Grapevine," *Harvard Business Review*, 1953, vol. 31, no. 5, pp. 43–49.

27. Davis, K.: "A Method of Studying Communication Patterns in Organizations," *Personnel Psychology*, 1953, vol. 6, pp. 301–312.

28. Deutsch, M.: "An Experimental Study of the Effects of Cooperation and Competition upon Group Process," *Human Relations*, 1949, vol. 2, pp. 199–231.

29. Elliott, J. D.: "Increasing Office Productivity by Job Enlargement," Report to the American Management Association, New York, Oct., 1953.

30. Ewing, T. N.: "A Study of Certain Factors Involved in Changes of Opinion," *Journal of Social Psychology*, 1942, vol. 16, pp. 63–88.

31. Festinger, L., and H. A. Hutte: "An Experimental Investigation of the Effect of Unstable Interpersonal Relations in a Group," *Journal of Abnormal & Social Psychology*, 1954, vol. 49, pp. 513–522.

32. Festinger, L., S. Schachter, and K. Back: *Social Pressures in Informal Groups*, Harper & Brothers, New York, 1950.

33. Festinger, L., and J. W. Thibaut: "Interpersonal Communication in Small Groups," *Journal of Abnormal & Social Psychology*, 1951, vol. 46, pp. 92–99.

34. Fiedler, F. E., et al.: "The Relationship of Interpersonal Perception to Effectiveness in Basketball Teams," Bureau of Research and Service, University of Illinois, Urbana, Ill., *Technical Report No. 3*, 1952.

35. Fiedler, F. E.: "Assumed Similarity Measures as Predictors of Team Effectiveness in Surveying," Bureau of Research and Service, University of Illinois, Urbana, Ill., *Technical Report No. 6*, 1953.

36. Green, N. E.: "Verbal Intelligence and Effectiveness of Participation in Group Discussion," *Journal of Educational Psychology*, 1950, vol. 41, pp. 440–445.

37. Greer, F. L.: "Interpersonal Knowledge and Group Effectiveness," *Journal of Abnormal & Social Psychology*, 1954, vol. 49, pp. 411–414.

38. Grinkler, R. R., and J. P. Spiegel: *Men Under Stress*, Blakiston Division, McGraw-Hill Book Company, Inc., New York, 1945.

39. Gross, E.: "Characteristics of Cliques in Office Organizations," *Research Studies*, State College of Washington, 1951, vol. 19, pp. 131–136.

40. Gross, E.: "Some Functional Consequences of Primary Controls in Formal Work Organizations," *American Sociological Review*, 1953, vol. 18, pp. 368–373.

41. Grossack, M. M.: "Some Effects of Cooperation and Competition upon Small Group Behavior," *Journal of Abnormal & Social Psychology*, 1954, vol. 49, pp. 341–348.

42. Halpin, A. W.: "The Leadership Behavior and Combat Performance of Airplane Commanders," *Journal of Abnormal & Social Psychology*, 1954, vol. 49, pp. 19–22.

43. Harvey, O. J.: "An Experimental Approach to the Study of Status Relations in Informal Groups," *American Sociological Review*, 1953, vol. 18, pp. 357–367.
44. Hemphill, J. K.: "Situational Factors in Leadership," Ohio State University, Columbus, Ohio, Personnel Research Board, *Leadership Studies No. 4*, 1949.
45. Hemphill, J. K.: "Group Factors in Leadership. I. Relations between the Size of the Group and the Behavior of 'Superior Leaders,'" *Journal of Social Psychology*, 1951, vol. 32, pp. 11–22.
46. Horowitz, M. W.: "Induction of Forces in Discussion Groups," *Human Relations*, 1951, vol. 4, pp. 57–76.
47. Horowitz, M. W., and N. Pastore: "Relationship of Motive to Author and Statement," *Science*, 1955, vol. 121, pp. 110–111.
48. Hovland, C. I., and W. Mandell: "An Experimental Comparison of Conclusion-drawing by the Communicator and by the Audience," *Journal of Abnormal & Social Psychology*, 1952, vol. 47, pp. 581–588.
49. Hovland, C. I., et al.: *Communication and Persuasion*, Yale University Press, New Haven, 1953.
50. Hurwitz, J. I., et al.: "Some Effects of Power on the Relations among Group Members," *Group Dynamics*, Chap. 32, Row, Peterson & Company, Evanston, Ill., 1953.
51. Jackson, J. M.: "The Effect of Changing the Leadership of Small Work Groups," *Human Relations*, 1953, vol. 6, pp. 25–44.
52. Jacobson, E., et al.: "The Use of the Role Concept in the Study of Complex Organizations," *Journal of Social Issues*, 1951, vol. 7, pp. 18–27.
53. James, J.: "An Experimental Study of Tensions in Work Behavior," *Publications in Culture and Society*, University of California Press, Berkeley, Calif., 1951, vol. 2, pp. 203–242.
54. Janis, I. L.: "Personality Differences Associated with Responsiveness to Fear-arousing Communication," *Journal of Personality*, 1954, vol. 23, pp. 154–166.
55. Jennings, E. E.: "Improving Supervisory Behavior," *Wisconsin Commerce Studies*, 1954, vol. 2, no. 1. (*See also* "Technique of Successful Foremanship," *Wisconsin Commerce Studies*, 1953, vol. 1, no. 4.)
56. Jones, E. E.: "Authoritarianism and the Perception and Evaluation of Leadership Attitude," *The American Psychologist*, 1953, vol. 8, p. 374.

57. Katz, D.: "Morale and Motivation in Industry," *Publication J2-2*, Survey Research Center, Ann Arbor, Mich., 1949.

58. Katz, D., et al.: *Productivity, Supervision and Morale in an Office Situation*, Institute for Social Research, Ann Arbor, Mich., 1950.

59. Katz, D., et al.: *Productivity, Supervision and Morale among Railroad Workers*, University of Michigan Press, Ann Arbor, Mich., 1951.

60. Katz, D., and R. L. Kahn: "Some Recent Findings in Human Relations Research," *Publication JJ-11*, Survey Research Center, Ann Arbor, Mich., 1952.

61. Kelley, H. H.: "The Warm-cold Variable in First Impressions of Persons," *Journal of Personality*, 1950, vol. 18, pp. 431–439.

62. Kelley, H. H.: "Communication in Experimentally Created Hierarchies," *Human Relations*, 1951, vol. 4, pp. 39–56.

63. Kelley, H. H., and E. H. Volkart: "The Resistance to Change of Group-anchored Attitudes," *American Sociological Review*, 1952, vol. 17, pp. 453–465.

64. Kretch, D., and R. S. Crutchfield: *Theory and Problems of Social Psychology*, McGraw-Hill Book Company, Inc., New York, 1948.

65. Laird, D. A., and E. C. Laird: *Sizing Up People*, McGraw-Hill Book Company, Inc., New York, 1951.

66. Laird, D. A., and E. C. Laird: *Practical Business Psychology*, Gregg Publishing Division, McGraw-Hill Book Company, Inc., New York, 1956.

67. Lanzetta, J. T.: "Group Behavior under Stress," *The American Psychologist*, 1953, vol. 8, p. 284; *Human Relations*, 1955, vol. 8, pp. 29–52.

68. Lauterbach, A.: *Man, Motives, and Money*, Cornell University Press, Ithaca, N.Y., 1954.

69. Lawrence, P. R.: "How to Deal with Resistance to Change," *Harvard Business Review*, 1954, vol. 32, no. 3, pp. 49–57.

70. Lawshe, C. H., and B. F. Nagle: "Productivity and Attitude toward Supervisor," *Journal of Applied Psychology*, 1953, vol. 37, pp. 159–162.

71. Leavitt, H. J., and R. A. H. Mueller: "Some Effects of Feedback on Communication," *Human Relations*, 1951, vol. 4, pp. 401–410.

72. Lee, I. J.: *How to Talk to People,* Harper & Brothers, New York, 1952.
73. Lewin, K.: "The Conceptual Representation and the Measurement of Psychological Forces," *Contributions to Psychological Theory,* vol. 1, no. 4, Duke University Press, Durham, N.C., 1938.
74. Lieberman, S.: "The Relationship between Attitudes and Roles: a Natural Field Experiment," *The American Psychologist,* 1954, vol. 9, pp. 418–419.
75. Likert, R., and R. Lippitt: "Modern Methods of Measuring Public Reaction and the Applications of These Methods to the Social Welfare Field," *Publication FF 1–6,* 1952, Institute for Social Research, Ann Arbor, Mich.
76. Lindgren, H. C.: *Effective Leadership in Human Relations,* Hermitage House, Inc., New York, 1954.
77. Lippitt, R., et al.: "The Dynamics of Power," *Human Relations,* 1952, vol. 5, pp. 37–64.
78. Lorge, I., et al.: "Comparison of Decisions Written by Large and Small Groups," *The American Psychologist,* 1953, vol. 8, p. 352.
79. Maccoby, N.: "The Relationship of Supervisory Behavior and Attitudes to Group Productivity in Two Widely Different Industrial Settings," *Publication J7–2,* 1949, Institute for Social Research, Ann Arbor, Mich.
80. Maier, N. R. F.: "An Experimental Test of the Effect of Training on Discussion Leadership," *Human Relations,* 1953, vol. 6, pp. 161–174.
81. Maier, N. R. F., and A. R. Solem: "Audience Role Playing: a New Method in Human Relations Training," *Human Relations,* 1951, vol. 4, pp. 279–295.
82. Maier, N. R. F., and A. R. Solem: "The Contributions of a Discussion Leader to the Quality of Group Thinking," *Human Relations,* 1952, vol. 5, pp. 277–288.
83. Mann, F. C.: "Work Satisfactions as a Function of the Discrepancy Between Inferred Aspirations and Achievements," *Publication 739,* 1953, Survey Research Center, Ann Arbor, Mich.
84. Mann, F. C., and H. Baumgartel: "Absences and Employee Attitudes in an Electric Power Company," Survey Research Center, 1952, Ann Arbor, Mich.
85. Mann, F. C., and H. Baumgartel: "The Supervisor's Concern with Costs," Survey Research Center, 1953, Ann Arbor, Mich.

86. Mann, F. C., and J. Dent: "Appraisals of Supervisors and Attitudes of Their Employees in an Electric Power Company," Institute for Social Research, 1954, Ann Arbor, Mich.

87. Mann, F. C., and J. K. Dent: "The Supervisor: Member of Two Organizational Families," *Harvard Business Review*, 1954, vol. 32, no. 6, pp. 103–112.

88. Massarik, F., et al.: "Sociometric Choice and Organizational Effectiveness, a Multi-Dimensional Approach," *Sociometry*, 1953, vol. 16, pp. 211–238.

89. May, R.: *The Meaning of Anxiety*, The Ronald Press Company, New York, 1950.

90. Miller, D. C., and W. H. Form: *Industrial Sociology*, Harper & Brothers, New York, 1951.

91. Mills, T. M.: "Power Relations in Three-person Groups," *American Sociological Review*, 1953, vol. 18, pp. 351–357.

92. Mintz, A.: "Non-adaptive Group Behavior," *Journal of Abnormal & Social Psychology*, 1951, vol. 46, pp. 150–159.

93. Mintz, A.: "The Failure of a Propaganda Campaign Attempting to Influence the Behavior of Customers in the National Interest by Predominatingly Selfish Appeals," *Journal of Social Psychology*, 1953, vol. 38, pp. 49–62.

94. Morse, N. C.: *Satisfactions in the White-collar Job*," University of Michigan Press, Ann Arbor, Mich., 1953.

95. Nagle, B. F.: "Productivity, Employee Attitude, and Supervisor Sensitivity," *The American Psychologist*, 1953, vol. 8, p. 408.

96. Osterberg, W. H.: "A Method for the Study of Bargaining Conferences," *Personnel Psychology*, 1950, vol. 3, pp. 169–178.

97. Pelz, D. C.: "Influence: a Key to Effective Leadership in the First-line Supervisor," *Personnel*, 1952, vol. 29, pp. 209–217.

98. Preston, M. G., and R. K. Heintz: "Effects of Participatory vs. Supervisory Leadership on Group Judgment," *Journal of Abnormal & Social Psychology*, 1949, vol. 23, pp. 345–355.

99. Radke, M., and D. Klisurich: "Experiments in Changing Food Habits," *Journal of the American Dietetic Association*, 1947, vol. 23, pp. 403–409.

100. Raven, B. H.: "Group Pressure toward the Selection and Distortion of Content in Communication and Cognition," *The American Psychologist*, 1953, vol. 8, p. 420.

101. Riesman, D.: *The Lonely Crowd*, Yale University Press, New Haven, Conn., 1950.

102. Roethlisberger, F. J., and W. J. Dickson: *Management and the Worker,* Harvard University Press, Cambridge, Mass., 1947.
103. Rose, A. M.: *Union Solidarity,* University of Minnesota Press, Minneapolis, Minn., 1952.
104. Rosenthal, D., and C. N. Cofer: "The Effect on Group Performance of an Indifferent and Neglectful Attitude Shown by One Member," *Journal of Experimental Psychology,* 1948, vol. 38, pp. 568–577.
105. Roy, D.: "Efficiency and 'the Fix': Informal Intergroup Pressures in a Piecework Machine Shop," *American Journal of Sociology,* 1954, vol. 60, pp. 255–266.
106. Schachter, S.: "Deviation, Rejection, and Communication," *Journal of Abnormal & Social Psychology,* 1951, vol. 46, pp. 190–207.
107. Schachter, S., et al.: "An Experimental Study of Cohesiveness and Productivity," *Human Relations,* 1951, vol. 3, pp. 229–238.
108. Scheidlinger, S.: *Psychoanalysis and Group Behavior,* W. W. Norton & Company, Inc., New York, 1952.
109. Sherif, M., and C. W. Sherif: "Groups in Harmony and Tension," Harper & Brothers, New York, 1953.
110. Sherif, M., et al.: "Status in Experimentally Produced Groups," *American Journal of Sociology,* 1955, vol. 60, pp. 370–379.
111. Smigel, O.: "Public Attitudes toward 'Chiseling' with Reference to Unemployment Compensation," *American Sociological Review,* 1953, vol. 18, pp. 59–67.
112. Staton, T. V.: "Relation of Selected Factors to Individual Prestige Achieved in Seminars," *The American Psychologist,* 1948, vol. 3, p. 267.
113. Steinzor, B.: "The Spatial Factor in Face-to-Face Discussion Groups," *Journal of Abnormal & Social Psychology,* 1950, vol. 45, pp. 552–555.
114. Stendler, C., et al.: "Studies in Cooperation and Competition: I. The Effects of Working for Group and Individual Rewards on the Social Climate of Children's Groups," *Journal of Genetic Psychology,* 1951, vol. 79, pp. 173–197.
115. Strupp, H. H., and H. J. Hausman: "Some Correlates of Group Productivity," *The American Psychologist,* 1953, vol. 8, pp. 443–444.
116. Sullivan, H. S.: *The Interpersonal Theory of Psychiatry,* W. W. Norton & Company, Inc., New York, 1953.

117. Survey Research Center: "Some Recent Findings in Human Relations Research," *Publication JJ–11*, 1952, Ann Arbor, Mich.
118. Thelen, H. A.: *Dynamics of Groups at Work*, University of Chicago Press, Chicago, 1954.
119. Thibaut, J.: "An Experimental Study of the Cohesiveness of Underprivileged Groups," *Human Relations*, 1950, vol. 3, pp. 251–278.
120. Thibaut, J., and J. Coules: "The Role of Communication in the Reduction of Interpersonal Hostility," *Journal of Abnormal & Social Psychology*, 1952, vol. 47, pp. 770–777.
121. Thompson, W. R., and R. Nishimura: "Some Determinants of Friendship," *Journal of Personality*, 1952, vol. 20, pp. 305–314.
122. Van Zelst, R. H.: "Empathy Test Scores of Union Leaders," *Journal of Applied Psychology*, 1952, vol. 36, pp. 293–295.
123. Van Zelst, R. H.: "Sociometrically Selected Work Teams Increase Production," *Personnel Psychology*, 1952, vol. 5, pp. 175–186.
124. Van Zelst, R. H.: "Validation of a Sociometric Regrouping Procedure," *Journal of Abnormal & Social Psychology*, 1952, vol. 47, pp. 299–301.
125. Viteles, M.: *Motivation and Morale in Industry*, W. W. Norton & Company, Inc., New York, 1953.
126. Walker, C. R., and R. H. Guest: *The Man on the Assembly Line*, Harvard University Press, Cambridge, Mass., 1952.
127. Welch, H. J., and G. H. Miles: *Industrial Psychology in Practice*, Pitman Publishing Corporation, New York, 1932.
128. Weschler, I. R., et al.: "Job Satisfaction, Productivity and Morale: a Case Study," *Occupational Psychology*, 1952, vol. 24, pp. 1–14.
129. Winn, A.: "Training in Administration and Human Relations," *Personnel*, 1953, vol. 30, pp. 139–149.
130. Wright, M. E.: "The Influence of Frustration upon the Social Relations of Young Children," *Character & Personality*, 1943, vol. 12, pp. 111–122.

Index